"REFERENCE WORK IN THE HUMANITIES"

Edmund F. SantaVicca

The Scarecrow Press, Inc.
Metuchen, N.J., & London 1980

Library of Congress Cataloging in Publication Data

SantaVicca, Edmund F   1947-
    Reference work in the humanities.

    1.   Reference services (Libraries)--Problems,
exercises, etc.   2.   Humanities--Library resources--
Problems, exercises, etc.   I.   Title.
Z711.2.S26   011'.02   80-18783
ISBN 0-8108-1342-4

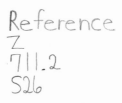

To

JERRY and BLANCHE

TABLE OF CONTENTS

INTRODUCTION   vii

PHILOSOPHY   1
    Questions   3
    Search Problems   12
    Case Studies   18

RELIGION AND MYTHOLOGY   25
    Questions   27
    Search Problems   36
    Case Studies   42

LITERATURE   49
    Questions   51
    Search Problems   60
    Case Studies   66

MUSIC   73
    Questions   75
    Search Problems   83
    Case Studies   89

FINE ARTS   97
    Questions   99
    Search Problems   108
    Case Studies   115

THEATER ARTS   121
    Questions   123
    Search Problems   135
    Case Studies   141

INTERDISCIPLINARY SEARCH PROBLEMS   147

APPENDIX   155

INTRODUCTION

The present volume has been designed for a number of audiences. Among these are the library educator, the student of library and information science, the practicing professional, and the paraprofessional. It is hoped that the library educator will find the exercises below a useful supplement to any pre-existing exercises, as well as a complement to any course syllabus designed to study basic information sources in the humanities. Similarly, it is hoped that through completing these exercises, the student of library and information science will have a better understanding of the complexities of reference work in those subject areas that comprise the humanities. Both the professional and the paraprofessional may make use of these same exercises as a means of getting to know the particular collection with which they must work and developing their own search strategies and skills, which play such an important part in the reference process.

To some extent these exercises are a reaction to my own education and my own teaching methods, the latter of these now firmly entrenched in a "continuous revision" policy. It has been my experience as both a student and a professor that too much emphasis is sometimes placed upon the nature and reference qualities of specific titles. I would hasten to add that I do not believe that such an emphasis should be eliminated, merely lessened; it should be complemented by a strong understanding of how the qualities of these titles come into play in the course of reference work. Concurrent with this, as an integral part of teaching reference work in any subject field, should be a greater understanding of that eclectic and amorphous entity that has come to be identified, sometimes euphemistically, as the patron. If upon completing a course in information sources in the humanities, one understood as much about patrons as about reference sources, perhaps this text would be substantially changed. But this is not the case; and so it is hoped that through these exercises one may realize that any degree of difficulty in carrying out reference work is to some extent affected by the particular patron who is being served.

vii

In addition to having a sound understanding of reference sources and the ability to analyze patrons and their requests, successful students of reference and reference librarians have both become aware of their own thought processes. That is to say, they are able to understand the language and thought processes that they, as individuals, are using to translate the language of the patron into the language of potential retrieval systems in their particular library settings. Again in the realm of my own experience, this is one of the most difficult areas of teaching reference work--helping students understand themselves and their individual abilities as they relate to the reference process.

The present exercises have been composed not as a panacea, but as a move in the right direction. Basically, these exercises have been divided into three arbitrary classifications: questions, search problems, case studies. All three are concerned with familiarizing readers with reference sources in the humanities; with familiarizing them with the disciplines that comprise the humanities; and familiarizing them with the difficulties and complexities of the patron and the reference interview. As will become evident after using these exercises for a period of time, virtually every rule of English grammar, capitalization, punctuation, and style has been violated. Such is the reality of life at the reference desk. Few patrons have developed the language skills necessary to simplify the reference process; and there is no need to pretend otherwise in the classroom.

Regarding the Questions sections of these exercises, instructions appear at the beginning of each. Basically, what is required is a complete bibliographic citation for at least one source that will answer each question listed in that section. I have also found it useful for students to record the initial search terms used in finding the answer, as this will often shed light upon individual thought processes. In addition, the entry term under which the student found the information should also be noted, for the purposes of comparison.

The Search Problems sections contain twenty exercises of a paragraph format, each centered on one subject area but demanding a variety of information on that subject which requires the utilization of more than one source in the provision of the answers. Of all the exercises, it is these that will probably appear to be the most garbled and confusing. And so they are. The initial assignment requested in each exercise is a reformulation or restatement of the question (or information desired) into comprehensible units. What does the patron really want to know? In some cases, due to clouding, the answer may be arbitrary. After this initial work has been completed, the exercise can proceed in the same manner as with the Questions. Again, some indication of search terms and entry terms should be made, along with a complete bibliographic citation for a source that will provide an answer. In those cases where the sources are too numerous to mention, indication may be made of how one would tell the patron to proceed independently in order to locate the desired information.

The Case Studies exercises are basically an amplification of the type of exercise found in the Search Problems. The notable differences are that one must use more and more varied sources to answer the questions; and that they are designed essentially to be divided among various members of the particular class using them, thus forming a unified classroom discussion centering on one subject. In comparison, the Search Problems have been designed so that each may be assigned to a different student, allowing for a slightly less homogeneous, yet valuable, classroom discussion. The Questions may be assigned either selectively or collectively in any number.

One final note regarding these exercises: many of them may seem artificial. Many, but definitely not the majority, are. Most of the exercises contained in this text have been adapted from actual classroom assignments and requests for information made either to myself or to friends and colleagues. It is only because they are phrased in a certain manner that this may not appear to be the case. As for the others, I believe that they are a valuable means of introducing the reader to certain aspects of the disciplines that comprise the humanities, and to the reference process in general. In the end, I suspect that many would be surprised to discover which are the adaptations and which are the creations.

It is with definite purpose that no syllabus or bibliography accompanies these exercises. To list all of the works that one might use in answering these exercises would produce a text longer than the work itself. Any list of information sources in the humanities should provide an adequate supply of titles that can be used in solving the exercises, but the nature of reference work is such that sources outside of a subject area, or more general sources, are sometimes needed. For this reason, I have tried to allow flexibility and adaptability of the exercises in relation to any syllabus or bibliography.

I encourage any reaction to the present text to be conveyed to the author. Suggestions for expansion and suggestions for omission are equally welcome.

Grateful acknowledgment is made to George Peabody College for Teachers of Vanderbilt University for the resources made available for the completion of this work. Special thanks to Mr. Jerry Waters for assistance in typing the final manuscript.

Nashville, Tennessee
December 1979

PHILOSOPHY

PHILOSOPHY

Questions

Please provide a complete bibliographic citation for at least one source that will provide an answer to each of the following questions.

1. Where could I locate a philosophical argument that proves that God does exist?

2. Explain the difference between materialism and capitalism.

3. What does the suffix "ism" mean?

4. At what point in time does life end and death begin?

5. Has the Society for Ancient Greek Philosophy published anything during the past five years?

6. Are there any libraries in the United States that have special collections on agnosticism?

7. Provide a complete bibliographic citation to two periodical articles written in the past three years on the subject of skepticism.

8. What are sexual ethics?

9. Is nudism a philosophy? Who founded the school?

10. How is William James ranked among the world's great philosophers?

11. What is the relationship between philosophy and psychology?

3

12. In 1949, Felice Battaglia's book titled Il problema morale nell'esistenzialismo was published. Who was the publisher? Was this the first edition?

13. I need to locate two or three books concerning the philosophy of Martin Buber.

14. Is Simone de Beauvoir considered to be more of a philosopher or more of a writer?

15. Who is the author of an article entitled "Albert Camus and the Ethics of Absurdity," which appeared in the 1965 volume of Ethics?

16. Who is considered to be the oldest philosopher known to man?

17. Why did Socrates commit suicide?

18. Peter Popoff wrote an article that appeared in the 1962 issue of Deutsche Zeitschrift für Philosophie (Berlin). What was the title of the article?

19. Are there any philosophical tracts that are still being written in Latin?

20. Do any concordances exist to the works of Blaise Pascal?

21. Is it all right to engage in premarital intercourse?

22. I want to know Leibniz' complete name, birth and death date, and the title of his most important work.

23. I would like to know the names of any philosophical associations or organizations in France that are specifically concerned with existentialism.

24. Who is the current president of the American Philosophical Association?

25. Who is considered to be the first significant American philosopher?

26. Who is considered to be the first significant female American philosopher?

27. How many colleges or universities in the Southeast offer the M. A. degree in philosophy?

28. Are there any major African philosophers?

29. Is Sigmund Freud a philosopher or a psychologist?

30. I remember reading something about the Yippees a few years back; and I'm trying to find out exactly what their philosophy was.

31. Valerie Solonas once wrote something called The S. C. U. M. Manifesto. What was S. C. U. M. ? What was the document about?

32. What is a soul?

33. What exactly does a deipnosophist believe in?

34. Did Franklin Delano Roosevelt ever make any comments about philosophy or philosophers?

35. I need to locate a definition of "politics" as it might be used by a philosopher.

36. Who are the principal philosophers of science?

37. What exactly is an entity?

38. What does the phrase "ontogeny recapitulates phylogeny" mean? Is it associated with a particular school of philosophy?

39. What is the title of a good basic textbook of philosophy?

40. What are the basic tenets of pantheism?

41. Is transcendentalism a philosophy or a religion?

42. Was there much of a difference between the philosophy of Plato and that of Aristotle?

43. With what field of philosophy is the name Boole associated?

44. What is the central idea of Bertrand Russell's Why I Am Not a Christian?

45. How important is Friedrich Ueberweg's Grundriss der Geschichte der Philosophie as a reference work?

46. Where could I locate a basic outline of the principal Greek philosophers?

47. How many individual philosophers are included in the Loeb Classical Library?

48. What is the best English translation of Plato's Republic?

49. What are the principal names associated with the French Enlightenment?

50. Is the Library of Liberal Arts series in philosophy still being published?

51. Does the Catholic University of America publish any philosophical books in series?

52. What is the latest edition of Masterpieces of World Philosophy in Summary Form?

53. What is the frequency of the Italian serial Bibliografia Filosofica Italiana?

54. Does the Société Française de Philosophie publish a journal? What is the title?

55. Which came first, the chicken or the egg?

56. How many separate journals bear the title Philosophical Quarterly?

57. Where could I write to get a copy of the Proceedings of the American Catholic Philosophical Association?

58. Have any presidents of the United States been considered outstanding philosophers?

59. When did the Revue des Sciences Philosophiques et Théologiques begin publication? Is it still being published?

60. Did Jean-Paul Sartre ever found a philosophical journal?

61. What is the address of the Society for the Philosophical Study of Dialectical Materialism?

62. Does the Detroit, Michigan, Public Library have any special collections of philosophy?

63. Does Loyola University Press publish a series of philosophy monographs?

64. What is the longest philosophical work known to man?

65. Who is considered to have written the definitive biography of Voltaire?

66. Did Ludwig Wittgenstein ever receive any awards?

67. What were the circumstances of the death of René Descartes?

68. With which philosophical school is the name Kierkegaard associated? Is he still living?

69. Are there any general books about philosophy that might be suitable for a high school senior?

70. Was Boethius a very important person in the history of philosophy?

71. What was the first work of philosophy published after the invention of printing?

72. Who wrote The Philosophy of Eating? Was it really a philosophical work?

73. Is The History and Social Influence of the Potato a philosophical or historical work?

74. Which libraries in this country have special collections of St. Thomas Aquinas?

75. How much is membership in the International Phenomenological Society?

76. Who is the Chairman of the Department of Philosophy at the University of Texas at Austin?

77. Where could I locate a good critical work about the philosophy of Kant?

78. In which language is the serial Soviet Studies in Philosophy written?

79. What is the Spanish equivalent of "dialectical materialism"?

80. Who are the major American philosophers of education?

81. How many editions of John Locke's Essay Concerning Human Understanding are currently in print?

82. Are "ontology" and "teleology" related terms?

83. With which general time period is the philosophy of Epicureanism associated?

84. How important a work is Susanne Langer's Philosophy in a New Key?

85. Was The Voices of Silence by André Malraux originally written in French? When was it first translated into English?

86. Did Bertrand Russell ever write any histories of philosophy?

87. What is "aesthetics"?

88. Are there any atlases of philosophy that might indicate which philosophers came from which country?

89. A work by Bernard Bosenquet titled A History of Aesthetics was reprinted in 1966 by Humanities Press. What was the date of the original publication? How many editions were published before the reprint edition?

90. Where could I locate abstracts of articles that have been written about the subject of morals?

91. What was the most important philosophical work of Friedrich von Schelling? When was it written?

92. Are there any separately published bibliographies of criticism of the works of John Dewey?

93. Are there any annotated bibliographies about John Stuart Mill?

94. Who are the principal philosophers associated with mathematical logic?

95. How many computerized data bases exist in the field of philosophy?

96. Where could I locate a good compendium of Oriental philosophy?

97. Why is "Etiquette" placed under "Ethics" in the Library of Congress Classification scheme?

98. Where could I locate a book review of Sarva-Darsana-Sangraha: A Bibliographical Guide to the Global History of Philosophy?

99. Did philosophy play an important role in the lives of the early American Indians?

100. Is The Tibetan Book of the Dead considered to be a philosophical work or a religious work?

101. How many angels really can dance on the head of a pin?

102. In 1970, Northwestern University Press published Themes from the Lectures at the Collège de France. Whose lectures were they? Who was the translator?

103. When and by whom was The Symposia Read at the Joint Session of the Aristotelian Society and the Mind Association at the University of Sussex, 11th to 13th July, 1969 published? Is it currently available for purchase?

104. Are there any good films or filmstrips about philosophy available for purchase that are suitable for a high school audience?

105. Who is the author of I Am an Impure Thinker?

106. Are there any published reports of the Conference on Studies of the Acquisition and Development of Values, which met in Washington, D. C. , some time in 1968?

107. Are there any good Japanese dictionaries of ethics?

108. Who are the principal individuals covered in the work Les moralistes francais au dix-huitième siècle?

109.   When was the Encyclopedia of Morals, published by
        Greenwood Press in 1969, originally published?

110.   Morality and Rational Self-Interest, edited by David
        Gauthier, was published in 1970 by Prentice-Hall.
        Was it part of a series?

111.   Were there any histories of ethics written in Spanish
        during the 1960's?

112.   Was The Individual and His Relation to Society as Re-
        flected in British Ethics published in both an American
        and a British edition? Is this a one- or two-volume
        work?

113.   Are there any teaching aids available for teachers of
        philosophy at the community college level?

114.   I need complete bibliographic information for a work
        by I. P. McGreal titled Problems of Ethics, published
        some time in the early 1970's.

115.   Who is the publisher and what is the price of Docu-
        mentation et disciplines philosophiques (1969)?

116.   How many collected works of Hegel were published
        during the 1970's? In how many different languages?

117.   Is the Editions Anthropos edition of the Oeuvres d'Au-
        guste Comte illustrated?

118.   How many titles have been published in the Northwest-
        ern University Studies in Phenomenology and Existen-
        tial Philosophy series?

119.   What are the principal philosophical journals of Port-
        ugal?

120.   How many libraries in the United States have complete
        holdings of the serial Philosophy and History?

121.   Have any of Ludwig Wittgenstein's works been trans-
        lated into Italian?

122.   What is the most comprehensive critical work about
        Buddhist ethics?

123.   Which is the most recent German edition of the collected works of Wilhelm Dilthey (1833-1911)?

124.   How many works about philosophy have been written by John Campbell Sharp?

125.   What are truth tables?   Are they very expensive?

PHILOSOPHY

Search Problems

A. I've noticed that there is an awful lot being written these days about management and administration, particularly as it applies to libraries and how they are being run. But one thing which I'm not exactly clear on is what the difference is between a philosophy of management and a theory of management. I have heard both terms used a lot in the various courses that I'm taking, but no one seems to make a real distinction when they use the two terms. Is there a difference? If there is, what would be a good example of a philosophy of library management versus a theory of library management?

B. I have to do a term paper for my course in logic, and the instructor said that we could choose any three philosophers and compare the contributions that they have made to the field of logic. Since the only other course I've had in philosophy was something on the history of great ideas, I'm a little confused. Since she got the idea that most people in the class didn't know beans about the subject, she gave us a few names to consider. She said to go to the library and look up their names and a brief history of their lives; and then we could decide which ones we wanted to study in further depth. Well, I don't want to study any of them in further depth, but this paper is due in three weeks, and I think she is going to be a tough grader. Anyway, I jotted down a few of the names-- Aristotle, Aquinas, Occam, Bacon, Galileo, Leibniz, Kant, and DeMorgan. Now what do I do? Where could I go to read a little something about their lives? Would that also include information about their contribution to the field of logic?

C. On one of my trips to foreign museums I remember seeing a painting titled The School of Athens and it had two people in it that the guide said were Plato and Aristotle. He

said that the artist had tried to illustrate the differences in
their philosophies by the way in which he painted them. That
seems a little strange to me, but I thought I would pursue it
when I got back to the States. Was this painting painted during the time that Aristotle and Plato lived? Did the artist
know them? All I remember from the tour was that one of
them was pointing up and the other one down. Does that
mean that one of them went to heaven? I really don't see
how you can tell anything about their philosophy from the
painting? Where could I find some sort of explanation of
their philosophy and how it relates to this painting?

D. You are the new serials librarian in a large undergraduate library. As part of your new assignment, the director
asks that you evaluate the current titles the library is receiving. She would also like you to suggest new titles that might
be added in a few areas not currently covered. One of these
areas is philosophy. The memo you receive requests that you
supply, with annotations, a list of the ten periodicals that
would be best to supplement an undergraduate curriculum.
In addition to the annotations, you must also rate the periodicals from one to ten, indicating the priority in which they
should be acquired. How would you proceed in supplying the
information? Which ten titles would you list?

E. I have to do a five-page paper comparing dadaism, ni-
hilism, absurdism, and surrealism, indicating those qualities
which they have in common and how they differ as philosophies. I must also indicate the dates during which these philosophies flourished, and who the philosophers were that advanced them as philosophies. I would like to know if they
were philosophies which held a positive view of the world,
and which areas of the culture were most heavily influenced
by them.

F. I'm trying to find out how many works of philosophers
have been published in any microformats. Also, I would like
to know how many works which are available in microformat
are also available in hard-copy editions for general purchase.
Is there any way to find out if there are any complete philosophical series which are published in microformat, and only
in microformat?

G. Etiquette has long been an area which I just do not understand. It all seems so stiff and formalized, and seems more
embedded in ritual than in serious consideration of treatment
of the other individual or individuals. What, if any, are the

basic philosophies underlying the whole concept of etiquette?
Are people so stupid that they actually have to read a book
that tells them how to treat another person? Who first started
the whole notion of etiquette? I know the names of Emily
Post and Amy Vanderbilt; but surely they were not the first
people to write about the subject. Were there rules of etiquette, for instance, back in ancient Greece and Rome? Who
composed those rules, and why did they do it?

H.   I have to write up a brief report which compares Utopia
and Nirvana, which my professor claims are worlds apart.
They don't seem so different to me, just different terms
which are used to mean the same thing. But how could I
find out who invented those terms, or when they were first
used? I'd also like to find out what the terms currently
mean, and whether or not they have changed meanings over
time. I'd also like to find out how many cities or towns in
this country have been named either Utopia or Nirvana.

I.   I'm planning on pursuing a graduate degree in philosophy,
and would like some information about various departments
that may exist around the country. The main area I'm interested in is the Southeast. How many graduate schools are
there in the Southeast that offer a Master's degree in philosophy? What is the size of the student body in those depart-
mental programs? Also, is there any way I can find out who
teaches at which school; and the general reputation of the
school and of the faculty?

J.   I'd like to find some information, if anything has been
published, about the parallels between individual philosophies
and individual lifestyles. I guess what I mean is ... do people's lifestyles really reflect the way they believe or think?
I've been reading some magazine articles lately about how
the generation of the sixties, as much as it scorned materialism and the quest for wealth, actually produced a generation of now older people who are more materialistic and
money-grubbing than any previous generation. What would I
look under in the card catalog or in something like Readers'
Guide to locate that information?

K.   I've been thinking about a term paper topic for a 20th-
century comparative literature course. Last year I read
Beckett's Waiting for Godot; and the professor has talked
some about existentialism and 20th-century continental literature. This year I've read Sartre's Nausea and Camus' The
Stranger, and I became interested in the philosophical aspects

of the two novels. Did Camus ever have any direct contact
with Sartre? Did he ever write any explicitly philosophical
works? Also, I was wondering where I could find a brief list
of basic philosophical works by Sartre and others on existentialism. One other problem--I don't read French as well as
I need to, so I'd prefer reading stuff that is written in English.

L. For my world history course, I have to give a fifteen-
minute oral report that talks about some aspect of the ancient
world, and how it came to influence an aspect of the modern
world. I decided that the area of law might be an interesting
subject to talk about, especially about how different philosophies of law developed, and who the major old philosophers
were who wrote up the different laws that people used to live
by. The cut-off date for my particular project is 500 A. D. ,
but I can go back as far as I want to. Is there any one book
that would cover that time period and that talks about nothing
but law? If not, what kind of books or articles should I look
for? I think that most of what I need will probably be about
ancient Greece and Rome, but I think there may be some people from Egypt or Persia or other places that I might want
to talk about. Also, if I wanted to find any pictures of laws
that were written down in old handwriting, where could I find
them?

M. I have always enjoyed reading biographies of famous people from previous centuries, and even a few from this century. I have read a fair amount of material about a number
of the kings and queens of England, and I am fascinated by
the type of personalities they were. So many of them were
so very different from what someone would expect a king or
a queen to be. One area I would like to know about, and
which does not seem to be covered all that much in most of
these biographies is: did the people who raised and educated
all the princes and princesses who later went on to become
kings or queens--did these people have definite ideas or philosophies about what a king or queen should be? I mean,
were there definite ideas about what a king or queen should
know in order to be a good ruler, or what they should do
with all their powers once they became rulers?

N. I have just finished reading an interesting biography of
Queen Christina of Sweden, and I am very intrigued by how
she attempted to bring outside cultural influences to the court
of Sweden during her lifetime. Somehow, it seems, she arranged to bring a number of great thinkers of the time from

a variety of countries. She also engaged a number of individuals abroad to purchase books and manuscripts which were
later to be shipped to Sweden for her personal development
and the intellectual development of the court. It would seem
that she must have had a master plan behind all of this, and
some ideas about what she hoped to accomplish. Has anything been written about her philosophies of culture? Obviously she must have thought that it would have a positive effect upon both herself and the people around her; but it seems
a little difficult to believe that someone in as remote a place
as Sweden was at the time would be able to carry on philosophical conversations with the likes of someone like Descartes. But apparently she did. Is there any way I could
locate exactly what Descartes' reactions were to the likes of
Christina?

O.   For my classics course, the instructor wants us to hunt
up book reviews of some of the works we will be reading during the semester. She gave me four titles of some older
works, and I have to try to find some reviews by Monday.
The titles are: Early Greek Philosophy, by J. Burnet; The
Greek Philosophers, by W. K. C. Guthrie; Plato and His
Contemporaries, by C. G. Field; and The Philosophy of Aristotle, by someone named Allan. She also wants us to note
how many editions of each work were published, and when.
Where can I get this information, and find book reviews about
these books?

P.   In six months, a conference on death and death therapy
is scheduled to meet for three days. Your friend, a social
worker who happens to believe in the therapeutic effects of
reading, and who knows your capabilities, asks you if you
would consider compiling two annotated bibliographies on subjects related to the conference. The first should be a com-
pilation of items that have been published within the past five
years on the subject of death and philosophies of the role of
the social worker in death therapy. The second should be an
annotated list of fiction (novels and short stories) that deals
with the subject from a philosophical and coping perspective.
How would you go about locating the information, and what
limitations if any would you place upon the project?

Q.   I'm doing some research on various professions and professional organizations, and one of the areas I would like to
explore is the ethics of various professions. Do most or all
professions have some sort of code of ethics that the profession adheres to? But do barbers or librarians or entertainers

or even construction workers have codes of ethics for their
professions? Where could I find copies of these codes, if
they exist; and dates of when they were written?

R. I'm thinking about maybe becoming a police officer, but
I thought that before I went on down and filled out an application that it might be better to come to the library to see if
you all had any information on what the nature of a police officer's job is. I think I know most of what they do, but in
case they ask me during an interview what I think about that,
it might be nice to have a little something to fall back on,
right? So I think maybe I'd like to find some information on
what the role of a police officer should be, and something
about what the role of a police officer is today. Have police
always been the same? Are there a lot of different ideas
about what a police officer should be, or how much respect
he should command, or anything like that?

S. For my high school history course, we are going to do
a display in four exhibit cases in the school's main hallway.
We finally agreed that it might be nice to just do a big map
of the world and indicate all the philosophies which developed
out of a certain country. Just my luck! I got India! Well,
what I need to do is find out what the major philosophies of
India are, and who the people are that wrote them. I also
need to locate photographs or pictures of those people which
I can have copied somewhere, and some basic stuff about
their lives, like when they lived and died and stuff like that.

T. I've always wondered about inventors and some of the
strange products which they have managed to push off on the
public. Things like the hula hoop, skateboard, aerosol cans,
even the automobile. How would I go about finding out what
the philosophies were of the people who invented these items?
Did they think that civilization would be the better for their
inventions? Also, with such things as the automobile--were
there any philosophies about how the invention should be used?
Or how it could make a person better? Were any of these
philosophies successful in selling the invention to the public?

PHILOSOPHY

Case Studies

I. I'm trying to get together a discussion group on abortion for our monthly club meeting, and already some of the members have refused to participate because they don't think that it's the type of thing that ought to be discussed. But there are enough of us who do want to discuss it; but we are all pretty generally agreed that we don't know as much about the subject as we ought to. So they sent me down here to the library to see what I could locate on the subject, and to bring back everything I could check out and carry with me. Since we have at least three weeks to get all the information we need, I don't feel rushed, but I do want to get as much information as possible, particularly a lot of different viewpoints on the subject. Essentially, this is what I would like to find out:

Since the subject seems to be a moral issue, it might be helpful to locate some variety of statements regarding the morality or the ethics of abortion?

I've noticed that one of the points of contention in most debates on abortion is whether or not the unborn fetus is actually a living person or not. Has much been written on that subject? Am I likely to find information like that in an encyclopedia or do you think I might have to use a medical textbook?

A lot of religious groups seem to be opposed to abortion. Are there any groups that sanction abortion? If so, what is the philosophy behind their statements?

What about doctors and nurses? Does the medical profession have any particular philosophy about abortion?

Obviously, it directly concerns a large number of

women in this country. How many of them have actually expressed how they feel about the whole notion of abortion, not as part of any religious group, but just as women?

And some people argue that it is not just a woman's decision; that a man should have some say as to whether or not a woman should have an abortion. Has anybody made any public remarks on that aspect?

In how many states of the United States is abortion legal?

What were the primary philosophies behind the passage of those laws?

Have any surveys been done, like opinion polls, which indicate how people in this country feel about the subject of abortion?

What about in other countries. If it is legal in any foreign countries, maybe I could find something to do with what they believe?

And speeches. Have any politicians or other public figures in this country taken any particular stance on the subject of abortion?

Why exactly is there so much debate over the subject?

II. I've noticed that the name of Andrew Carnegie comes up a lot, especially in terms of public libraries. I guess that is because he gave such a large amount of money for the construction of public library buildings in the United States. But all people ever talk about are his buildings and his money. Nobody seems to know what the man behind the money was like, or why he gave it all to libraries instead of giving it to some other group or spending it all himself. Anyway, I have to do a paper for one of my education courses, dealing with some historical aspect of libraries. Since the professor said we could do one on individuals who were important to the field of librarianship, I thought that trying to get information on Carnegie might be interesting.

I'm not sure where to begin to look to find the information. Do you think that a general encyclopedia like Britannica or Americana would give me much information? I really want more than just biographical information, but I do want some of the details of Carnegie's life, to see if maybe there was something in his background that influenced his gifts to libraries.

Where and when was he born?

Was his family wealthy or was he one of those people who worked himself to death becoming a millionaire?

What kind of education did he have as a child?

Are there any sorts of records about the libraries he may have used as a child?

I'd also like to get at some of his philosophies of life, if there is any way to get at that.

Did he have a philosophy of life?

Or money, did he have any particular thoughts about money, and who should have it, and what they should do with it?

Maybe I could locate some of the information in dedication speeches, if he ever made any. Is there any record of any speeches he made at the openings of some of his library buildings?

Did Andrew Carnegie have any thoughts or philosophy about what a library should be?

What about architecture? Since most of his buildings all look alike, I wonder if he believed that that was the only way a library should look.

How many buildings did Andrew Carnegie donate?

Is there any way of judging what the impact of those gifts were to the communities to which he gave them?

Was he ever recognized during his lifetime by the library profession?

Did he have any influence at all over any of the philosophies of librarianship which exist today?

Did he know any librarians?

I don't imagine that there is too much written about him, but I sure would like to rely upon something more than an encyclopedia. Has anyone written any articles or books which could answer some of my questions?

Is there any way to tell from reading a book or an article about him as to whether or not the author likes or doesn't like him; or whether he agrees or disagrees with what Carnegie did?

Maybe I could find more information in any obituaries that were printed when he died. When did he die, and where do you think the best place would be to look to find a long obituary that praised him, and maybe explained his philosophy?

III.   I'm taking a course in women's studies and would like to gather some miscellaneous information for classroom discussion. The teacher suggested that we go out and explore some subjects which were of interest to us, and then come back to class with a list of suggestions of topics that we would like covered during the course of the semester. I know a little about women, but not nearly as much as I would like. Right now, I think I'd like to find information about feminism, particularly in this country. I realize that it is a big area, but I did make some notes about specific questions that I would like answered and/or discussed in class. Can you give me any help finding the answers? And if I just want to thumb through the card catalog, what words would I look under--Feminism? or are there better terms for what I want to find?

Is feminism a philosophy?

Can it be subscribed to by men?

Is there a difference between feminism and women's rights?

What is feminist socialism? Is it part of any feminist philosophies, or is it some sort of political concept?

Do all women basically feel good about being women?

Do most of them feel that they need more rights than those that they have now?

Who is considered to be the first American feminist?

Who were the major feminist philosophers in the United States during the nineteenth century?

What are considered to be the ten most significant feminist literary works ever written? Were they all written by women?

What is the relationship between feminism as a philosophy and the Equal Rights Amendment?

Are all women who support the Equal Rights Amendment feminists?

What about the Equal Rights Amendment and the philosophies behind that? Has anyone written any philosophical statements dealing with ERA, like how it might or might not change the status of women in this country?

Have any men written anything philosophical about the status of women in our society, either what it is now or what it could be?

Do women basically have different philosophies about life than men do?

Is there any way to find out how women's philosophies have changed since they were given the right to vote? Or how men's philosophies have changed since that time?

Has anyone done any studies analyzing the growth of industrialization in this country with the growth of feminism as a philosophy or as a lifestyle?

Do women currently have more power than they have ever had?

In what areas do women currently have the most power?

Which group has more individual sexual power, men or women?

I know there are at least a few small publishers of feminist books. How could I find out how many feminist presses there are in this country? Do they do much business? Who are the best-selling feminist authors? What kind of books do they write?

Are there any feminist books for children or young
adults? Do any of them explain feminism on an elementary
level, or are most of them novels?

IV. A group of us are meeting in about a week to start
planning the strategies of an anti-nuclear demonstration which
we plan to hold in about two months. Since part of the demonstration will be tables with leaflets and stuff explaining the
hazards of nuclear power, I'd like to gather up as much miscellaneous information about the subject as I could. You
know, the type of thing that the general public ought to know
about the dangers involved. What I would really like to get
at are speeches that people have made about the pros and
cons--especially the cons of nuclear power production. And
also some ideas about the dangers of war versus the scientific
advances that such power production might produce.

Where could I locate any anti-nuclear speeches which
have been made in the past five years or so, especially those
made by respected scientists and philosophers?

I would also like to locate some classic statements
from philosophers of all times about war and peace, and the
potential dangers that man constantly poses to himself. Is
stuff like that easy to find?

Did Plato or Socrates or any of those really ancient
people have anything profound or inspirational to say about
mankind and war, or anything about aggression versus non-
aggression?

I suppose a lot of this might be political as well, so
it might be helpful to track down some political philosophy
on the subject, if there is any. Could I do that easily?

Who was responsible for nuclear power in the first place?

Is there any way I could find out what that person
thought about what he was doing, and what sort of effect his
discovery was going to have on the future of the world, both
in terms of people and also in terms of the environment?

This is just such a large issue that it seems like
everyone must have something to say about it ... some sort
of opinion either for or against it. What about the general
public? How do they feel?

Are there any recorded interviews with the people who live around Three Mile Island? Or interviews with other people who live near other nuclear power plants?

Some illustrations might be helpful too, for the leaflets. Where could I find some really clear photos of nuclear power plants, both the inside and the outside?

And what about employees of these power plants? Do they have any thoughts or misgivings about their work situation? Don't they feel that they are endangering their lives as well as the lives of millions of other innocent people?

Most of what I have read on the subject so far has been in newspapers or magazines. Have any books been published which maybe collect a bunch of different people's thoughts about this issue?

Would it be possible to locate a chronology of nuclear mishaps?

I think I should also be aware of how much energy nuclear power promises to produce for the future. How likely is it to become the most important source of energy in the next century?

Wouldn't people be better off exploring the possibility of using the sun as a source of energy?

RELIGION AND MYTHOLOGY

RELIGION AND MYTHOLOGY

Questions

Please provide a complete bibliographic citation for at least
one source that will provide an answer to each of the following questions.

1. Who invented the Christmas tree? When was it first
   used as a religious symbol?

2. In what order were the four Gospels written?

3. What is the Nation of Islam?

4. How many churches in this country have Sunday School
   programs?

5. Next to the Pope, who holds the most power in the
   Vatican?

6. Do the Children of God publish a national magazine?

7. Is The Robe a Christian novel?

8. Who was Father Divine?

9. Which is the best biography of Aimee Semple McPher-
   son?

10. How many different gods are there?

11. Do Mormons still practice polygamy?

12. Is Santa Claus a religious figure?

13. Are there any journals published in English that deal exclusively with the subject of mythology?

14. How old are the Vedic myths?

15. What is the difference between Roman and Greek Catholicism?

16. How many Jewish holidays are celebrated in the United States?

17. In which language were the original texts of Buddhism written?

18. When did Joan of Arc become a saint?

19. How many religious newspapers are published in Nashville, Tennessee?

20. Which religion of the world has the most believers?

21. What is Zionism?

22. Does anyone still believe in Zoroastrianism?

23. Have any articles recently been published about vampires?

24. Are unicorns male or female?

25. When was the Reformation?

26. Why is birth control a religious issue?

27. Where could I find a review of The Passover Plot?

28. How many articles have been written in the past year on the subject of celibacy?

29. Who is the chief administrator of Catholic Schools in Lansing, Michigan?

30. Where could I locate information about a shrine to virginity that exists in Santa Fe, New Mexico?

31. Which religion has the most private schools in the United States?

32. What is the major religion in Greenland?

33. What is the significance of the menorah?

34. What is the most scholarly biography of Martin Luther?

35. Is Tai Chi a religious experience?

36. Did Jonathan really love David?

37. What is the best-selling religious phonorecord to date?

38. Are there any American saints?

39. How many different religions are covered in Sacred Books of the East?

40. What were the major issues in the Methodist church during 1977?

41. Where could I locate a map of Jerusalem that indicates various sites of religious significance?

42. How many times is love mentioned in the Bible?

43. When and where was the first church built in this country?

44. I heard that Frank Sinatra had a church built in Palm Springs, in memory of his mother. What is the name of it?

45. Where could I find a lengthy discussion of the phoenix as a mythological creature?

46. Are there many giants in Nordic mythology?

47. Where could I find a decent summary of the creation legends of the Aztecs?

48. What is the oldest legend in the world?

49. In how many languages is Watchtower published?

50. Who were the Pharisees?

51. Who founded the charismatic movement?

52. Who is the most famous goddess in Norse mythology?

53. How many nationally syndicated religious television programs are there?

54. Where do you go to become a rabbi?

55. How many different kinds of Baptists are there?

56. What does a crucifix signify?

57. Who was Helen P. Blavatsky?

58. Are there any good filmstrips about the Old Testament?

59. What makes an orthodox church orthodox?

60. Who is the largest publisher of religious monographs in the United States?

61. Does a pyramid have a religious significance?

62. For an Episcopalian wedding ceremony, on which side of the church should the groom's family be seated?

63. How much is Billy Graham worth?

64. How many nuns are there in the world?

65. What is the difference between a bar mitzvah and a bas mitzvah?

66. Are there any religious board games?

67. What is transubstantiation? Who believes in it?

68. I need a genealogical chart of the ancient Greek gods.

69. Are there any good dictionaries of non-classical mythology?

70. Which libraries in this country have special collections on American Indian mythology?

71. Of all the Egyptian gods, who had the most power?

72. Does the asphodel have any significance in mythology?

73. How many children did Europa have?

74. Why are there so many revivals in this country?

75. Is Shintoism practiced anywhere other than in Japan?

76. Which is the oldest Oriental religion?

77. What is the largest religious association in the world?

78. What was the first hymn printed in America?

79. How big is heaven?

80. How often does the American Theological Library Association meet?

81. Where could I find a social history of the Jews?

82. Is witchcraft a religion?

83. I would like to find a review of The Sacred Fire: The Story of Sex in Religion, by B. Z. Goldberg (1931).

84. Where could I find a commentary on the Epistles?

85. Has the Society for the Propagation of the Gospel published anything in the past five years?

86. What are the major written sources of Japanese mythology?

87. Who was the head of the House of Cadmus?

88. Where could I find a review of the Larousse Encyclopedia of Mythology?

89. Where could I locate a scholarly study of Arthurian legend and its influence on Celtic mythology?

90. Have any collections of African mythologies been published?

91. In addition to Myth and Ritual in Christianity, what other books has Alan Watts written about mythology?

92. How many books have been written about the Cult of Dionysus?

93. Which libraries in this country have special collections on the Anabaptists?

94. When was the Ecclesiae Occidentalis Monumenta Iuris Antiquissima, edited by C. H. Turner, published?

95. Where could I locate abstracts of articles written in French during the past year, dealing with the subject of hagiography?

96. Are there any comprehensive bibliographies of religion in Turkey?

97. What is the largest-circulating religious monthly magazine in the United States?

98. Does the Salvation Army publish any monographs?

99. Which libraries in this country subscribe to Gnostica News?

100. What is sin?

101. Where could I find pictures of what Jesus really looked like?

102. I need the title of a good introductory textbook on the history of religions.

103. Where is the headquarters of the Church of Jesus Christ of Latter Day Saints?

104. Where could I find a diagram or chart explaining the organization of the Unitarian Church in America?

105. What was the importance of William James' Varieties of Religious Experience?

106. In which language is the Talmud written?

107. Are any mythological tales or legends available on phonorecords or magnetic tape?

108. In 1950, H. J. Wechsler wrote Gods and Goddesses in Art and Legend. Is this work illustrated?

109. Have there been many articles published in French during the past five years on the subject of mythol-

ogy in literature?

110. Where could I find an illustration of what the goddess Diana looked like?

111. Are there any good educational films about Chinese mythology, suited for 10th-graders?

112. Where is the Maori heitiki?

113. Do elves really exist?

114. I would like to locate some materials on teaching religion effectively. Have there been any recent articles or books written about the subject?

115. When was the first edition of the Teachings of Swami Balananda published by Bhargava Press?

116. Who is the compiler of Heavenly Humor for All God's Children, published in 1975?

117. What is the mailing address of the Society for the Scientific Study of Religion?

118. How many people are members of the Church of Scientology?

119. Why is the Harvard Theological Review published by the University of Montana?

120. How much is a subscription to the Journal of Ecumenical Studies?

121. What is the intended reading audience of Christianity Today, a bi-weekly publication?

122. How many religious indexes index Zygon: Journal of Religion and Science?

123. Where could I locate a comprehensive list of religious periodicals published in the English language?

124. Which Jewish periodical has the largest circulation figures in the United States?

125. Who publishes The Catonsville Roadrunner, a Christian revolutionary serial that is published in London?

126. Where could I locate editorial reaction to the visit of the Pope to the United States?

127. Did Karl Marx ever write anything about religion?

128. Where could I locate some annotated bibliographies of juvenile fiction dealing with religious subjects?

129. Where could I find a list of books or articles written about mythologies concerning the sun?

130. Are there any annual conferences concerned with mythology or the study of mythology?

131. Is Superman a legend, a folk hero, or a mythological person?

132. Were people allowed to get divorced during Biblical times?

133. How many tribes of Israel are mentioned in the Bible?

134. Which is the most recently published version of the Bible?

135. Does a cantor need any special training?

136. Is liturgical drama still performed in the United States?

137. Of which profession is St. Jerome the patron saint?

138. Is Confucianism a religion?

139. Where could I find a list of Anglican textbooks for children?

140. Has anything been written recently on evangelism in Germany?

141. I need to locate some information on religious trusts.

142. How many religious books has Dale Evans written?

143. Of what significance were the Kahunas in Hawaiian mythology?

144. Who published the reprint edition of An Introduction

into the Science of Comparative Mythology and Folklore (1883)?

145. Is there an American edition of The Feathered Ser-
pent, by R. E. Robinson (1956)?

146. Are there any Polish mythologies?

147. When and where was Grensgebied, by K. H. Miskotte,
published? In what language is it written?

148. I need complete ordering information for a book called
Christian Rationalism and Philosophical Analysis.

149. Are there any good Swedish histories of religion?

150. Who translated The Elementary Forms of Religious
Life, by Emile Durkheim?

151. Has anyone written anything about the relationship of
religion and astronautics?

152. Where could I locate an extensive list of books about
church music?

153. Is the liturgy of the Methodist church pretty much the
same as Episcopalian liturgy?

154. Where could I locate a few short poems about cruci-
fixion?

155. How many dissertations have been written on the subject of ecclesiology?

156. In 1953, Pierre André wrote L'Asie menace, l'Afrique
attend. Who wrote the preface to this work?

157. Which is the best "reader in comparative religion"
available for purchase?

158. Are there any microtexts of the Bible?

159. Have any psychological biographies been written about
Judas Iscariot?

160. Where could I find information on the publication and
distribution of religious literature in the United States?

RELIGION AND MYTHOLOGY

Search Problems

A.   Browsing through the bookstore I shop at, I have noticed
that there seem to be more and more titles appearing in
print on the subject of the occult, or black magic, or various other types of cults.   Is this true?   Or is it just that
the bookstore has decided to stock more titles than usual in
this area?   Is there a renewed and growing interest in the
occult in the United States, or have people in this country
always been interested in the subject?   Are there many people in this country who practice the rituals that are written
about in these books?   Do they consider themselves to be religious people?   Do they look at these cults as religions, or
do they just see them as phases that they are going through?
What are the origins of black magic?

B.   Our family is going to go to the southwestern United
States for a three-week vacation in a motor home and we
would really like to make a point of stopping at various religious shrines in the areas we will be visiting, particularly
Arizona, New Mexico, and western Texas.   Where could we
find out where these shrines are?   It does not have to be
any particular shrine, but can be anything from chapels and
grottoes to souvenir stands.   Are there any books here in
the library that might have some photographs of these places,
so we could plan our route in advance?   What is the most
heavily visited shrine in the United States?   In the Southwest?

C.   I remember as a little boy that I used to really enjoy
reading stories about the Vikings and all the wonderful ad-
ventures that they would carry out.   And the thing I remember best is that everybody always seemed so devoted to the
gods.   It almost seemed as though the gods controlled their
lives, their every movement.   Was that really the case?   Did
the Vikings actually live their lives according to how the gods
thought they should?   I wish I had saved some of those novels,

but I no longer have any of them. Is there any way I could
get a list of books about Vikings that were written for children, and published in the early 1950's? I sure would like
to be able to reread some of those novels again.

D. I have to do a short paper on the god Zeus, detailing
all of the various forms, e.g., different animals, that he
took in order to seduce women. I have absolutely no idea
how to find that information, but the instructor said that I
could not change my topic. Since I have not read too many
stories about Zeus, or much mythology in general, I have no
idea even where this would be mentioned. Are there any books
here that could help me with the project? I also have to
make note as to whether Zeus just seduced women, or whether
he actually married any of them. Is it possible for a god to
marry a mortal?

E. My friend says that food which is sold in food stores for
Jews is marked by a letter U inside of a circle. I thought
Jewish food was labeled "kosher" so as to distinguish it from
non-Jewish food. Now I am confused. What is meant by
"kosher" food; and what does the symbol U inside of a circle
mean? I thought the symbol had something to do with a work
union, maybe, or maybe with the production of the food itself.
Also, do all Jewish people eat "kosher" food all the time or
only during special holy days?

F. For my high school course in comparative religions, I
need to find out how many different places there are in the
United States where a girl can go to become a nun; and how
many places there are where a man can go if he wants to be
a priest or a minister or whatever the title is in other religions. Do all religions in this country have nuns? Are
there different kinds of nuns or are they all the same? And
finally, I need to know which religions still require a vow of
chastity or celibacy?

G. My Sunday School teacher insists that there are only two
versions of the Bible--the right version and the wrong version.
I'm a little confused because the Bible that we use for Sunday
School says something about King James on the inside cover;
but I checked the two that we have at home and only one of
them says that on the inside. The other one says American
Standard Version at the bottom of the first page. How do I
know which one is right? And what makes a Bible right or
wrong?

H. I would like to buy some nicely written books which tell
some of the stories of the Old Testament as birthday pre-
sents for my nine-year-old niece and my twelve-year-old
nephew. I do not want to spend a lot of money, but I really
do want to find a few which have exceptional illustrations,
and which are written for a child or adolescent. Is there
anything that you could recommend?

I. I just moved to a new neighborhood, and it seems that
a lot of my neighbors are Catholics. The women in particular have mentioned something about a rosary or something
like that. When I asked one of them what it was, she just
showed me this thing that looked like a necklace; and it had
a cross at the end of it. Well, now that I know what it looks
like, I want to know what you do with it, but I'm too embar-
rassed to ask any of them. Does every Catholic have one?
And what do they use it for?

J. You are the new serials librarian in a large undergraduate library. As part of your new assignment, the director
asks you to evaluate the current titles the library is receiving. She would also like you to suggest new titles that might
be added in a few areas not currently covered. Since the
college in question has no formal courses in religion, the library has long been lax in acquiring journals and magazines
in this area. The memo you receive requests that you supply, with annotations, a list of the ten periodicals in the field
of religion that would be best to supplement an undergraduate
education. In addition to the annotations, you must also rate
the periodicals from 1 to 10, indicating the priority with
which they should be acquired. How would you proceed in
supplying the information? Which ten titles would you list?

K. I'm interested in going to college, and very interested
in receiving a degree with a major in religion or religious
studies. My problem is that I do not want to go to a college
that has any particular religious affiliation. It does not matter if it is a private school, as long as it is not owned or
run by a church. What are my options in the state of Michigan? Are there many schools, public or private, that grant
degrees in religion? What kind of a degree is it? A B.A. ?
I would like to go to a fairly small school, but also one where
the faculty has some sort of reputation in the field of religion.
Since I'm already thinking about going on for graduate work
at some point, I would want to make sure that the education
I receive as an undergraduate is sound, and would be recognized as good by any graduate school in the country.

L.   Our local minister recently put on display a number of
hymnals which he has collected over the years, and some
which he had borrowed from friends and other ministers. The
selection of about twenty is quite striking.   I am amazed at
the differences in their size, thickness, and the type of printing.   Some of the hymnals could fit into the palm of your
hand, while others would have to be carried with both hands.
I always thought that hymnals were all basically the same,
but I guess not.   Are there any books that explain the history of hymnals, and that might show some other examples?
What was the size of the smallest hymnal ever made? What
about the largest?   Do different religions put out their own
hymnals, which have to be approved by the headquarters of
the church?

M.   I want some information on the nation of Israel, and the
Jewish people.   I guess I don't understand or know exactly
what the history of the Jews is all about, because I am un-
clear as to how they could have all started out in one place,
ended up all over the world, and now they all want to go back
to Israel and make it an entirely Jewish country.   What is
the earliest historical record of the Jewish people?   Did they
actually start off in the area that is now known as Israel?
What did it used to be called?   What does the name Israel
mean?   Is it a Jewish word?   And how did it happen that the
Jews were dispersed all over the world?   Are there any maps
that might show, historically, the movement of the Jews over
the centuries?   When was Israel founded as a nation?   Didn't
that create problems with other nations having to give up land?
Does Israel see itself as a political or religious state?   How
many people live there now?   Since it is such a small country, how easily will it be able to grow?   How do Jews generally feel about non-Jews in Israel?

N.   My mother has mentioned that a few of our great-great-
uncles were circuit-riding preachers for the early Methodist
church in the United States; and she has come up with some
very funny stories about some of them.   Some of the stories
I think might be true; but some of them just sound too strange
to be true.   I have their names here with me, and I'd like
to know if there are any books in the library which might
make some mention of them ... like a Who's Who or something like that.   I would also like to find any books you might
have on the nature of the work of circuit-riding preachers in
general, to see if some of the stories my mother has told
me were true or not.

O.   My husband and myself are planning a trip to Europe

over the Christmas holidays, and I would like to know, before
we finalize our itinerary, if there are many religious festivals occurring during that period of time.   Since we will probably be traveling primarily through France, Spain, Germany,
and Poland, those are the countries I'm interested in knowing
more about.   I would think that since Spain has a lot of Catholics, there are probably a number of festivals or celebra-
tions there; but I'm just not sure about the other countries.
Are France and Germany and Poland predominantly Catholic?
I saw something on the news about how the churches in Poland had to hold their services in hidden places.   Is that
true?   Does that mean that they do not have any public festivals to celebrate Christmas?   Is there any single listing or
calendar of religious festivals in those countries?

P.   I've just finished reading The Exorcist, and it really has
got me interested in the whole idea of devil-possession and
exorcism.   Can you tell me if people have always had to be
exorcised; I mean, has the devil or some other evil spirit
always been around, taking possession of people's bodies and
souls?   What kind of training does a person have to have to
be an exorcist?   Can only priests or ministers do it, or
could somebody like me develop the necessary skills?   How
do the various Christian churches feel about exorcism?   Does
it always work?   What happens if it does not?   What about
the non-Christian churches; are there some sort of exorcism
rites in those churches, too?

Q.   Where could I find a well-written explanation and discussion of the sacraments of the Christian church?   What I'm
particularly interested in knowing is whether or not Protes-
tants and Catholics have the same sacraments (and the same
number of sacraments).   Also, I would like to know what the
significance of each of the sacraments is.   Does a person
have to receive all the sacraments to be a total Christian?
What exactly is Extreme Unction?   Does any other church,
Christian or non-Christian, recognize this as a sacrament?

R.   I have to give a short speech for a religion class on the
notion of heaven and hell in Oriental religions.   Basically,
I need to know whether all or any of the Oriental religions
had any beliefs in the notion of a heaven or a hell, and what
they called their equivalent of it.   I would also like to be
able to locate any textual descriptions of the kind of places
these were.   What were the qualifications for getting into
their heaven, or their hell?   Did they also have some sort
of concept of a purgatory or a limbo, or was it just a heaven

or a hell, or nothing at all? It would probably help my grade if I could find some good illustrations, done by artists of those faiths, of heaven or hell. Where could I find some?

S. I am interested in finding some information on Iran, and what has been happening there over the past few years, from a religious perspective. Is all of the civil disorder which has taken place there a result of the politics of the country, or the conflicts of various religious groups? Was the Shah of Iran considered to be a spiritual leader as well as a political leader? Also, the man who replaced him--I can't remember his name, but he seems to be more of a religious leader than a head of state--does he want to make the entire country follow his religious beliefs? Or does all the country already do that? How many different religions are there in Iran? I've also noticed that there have been a lot of executions taking place there since this new man came to power. Is killing sanctioned by his religion?

T. For my high school social studies course, I have to do a report on something to do with American Indians. I decided to do something about Indian religion, and especially about medicine men and what they did. Were medicine men priests or did they just have magical powers? What kind of training did they have? Who were the most famous medicine men among the Indians? Where could I get some pictures of what some of them looked like? Are there any medicine men still living today?

U. I am doing a class report on the history of popes in the Roman Catholic Church. Where can I find out how many popes there were? Were any of them married? Did any of them have any children? Were any of them saints, too? How does a pope become a pope? Are there any special requirements? Who is the current pope; and for how long has he held this position? Also, what is a papal bull?

RELIGION AND MYTHOLOGY

Case Studies

I. Each year, shortly after Halloween, the Charring Cross
Reformed Baptist Church Sunday School begins planning the
annual Christmas pageant, which will take place on Christmas
Eve. Because the event has been well received for the past
five years, not only within the church congregation but among
the entire town population, it was decided at the finish of
last year's pageant that "educational seminars" would be held
this year, for the purpose of promoting knowledge and aware-
ness about various aspects of Christmas, Christianity, and
the development of ritual and hymns within the Baptist tradi-
tion.

So that the organizers (lay people from the congregation) of
these seminars could adequately anticipate exactly what it is
that people are most interested in, a brief questionnaire was
circulated among the group that attended last year's pageant,
with instructions to list questions that people would like to
have answered and discussed as part of the seminars. Due
to the great diversity of the population and congregation, particularly in terms of age and educational level, it was thought
best simply to divide the questionnaire into four sections:
Christmas, Christianity, Ritual, and Hymns. As it turned
out, the vast majority of the questions focused upon Christmas.

Since the church itself maintained a small library with works
written primarily for church officers, it would be futile for
the members of the Sunday School to search there for the
answer to these questions. The only solution was to pay a
visit (en masse) to the Charring Cross Public Library (100,000
volumes). The following Saturday, seven members of the
class descended upon their favorite librarian, with a few of
the questions they thought to be most interesting. After looking at the list of some thirty-odd questions, the librarian

thought it best to organize them into some sort of pattern by topic, so that each student could pursue a different path of sources. As this initial sorting process took place, it was evident that some of the questions could be answered relatively easily, and that others would involve a more in-depth search.

Following is a sampling of the questions presented. What would your search strategy be for arriving at the answers, and which sources would seem most likely to supply the information being sought?

How many people were present when Jesus was born?

Was Jesus really a White man? Somebody told me he was Black.

What were the real names of the three wise men who came to visit the baby Jesus? Were they Baptists? Why were they called Magi?

Did it snow the night that Jesus was born?

Are there any maps that indicate the exact location of the Nativity?

What is the Nativity? Why is it called that?

How many angels are there in heaven?

What is Immaculate Conception? How did Joseph meet Mary?

How far did Jesus' parents travel after they left Egypt for not paying taxes?

Where is Jerusalem, and who owns it, or runs it now? Where could I find some pictures of how it looked at the time of Jesus' birth, and how it looks now?

Have there been any good movies made lately about the life of Jesus?

What is frankincense? myrrh? Can I get any locally?

Who was the pope when Jesus was born?

Which day of the week was Jesus born? What was the exact date?

Why did his parents name him Jesus? Does the name mean anything?

What was the average yearly income in Egypt at the time?

What was the tax rate?

What kind of music was played during this period? Are there any pictures available of the instruments?

Are Jesus and Santa Claus related?

Where was John the Baptist when Jesus was born? How old was he?

II.   Last week we had some guest speakers for my human development course. Since the topic for the day was supposed to be "Aspects of Human Sexuality," my instructor invited some homosexuals to come to class and talk about their sexuality and their lifestyles. Well, I just could not believe it. One of them was a minister or pastor for a local church which I did not even realize existed. It's called Metropolitan Community Church ... and I guess it is a Gay church. Since the class was more concerned about sexuality than religion, we really did not have the time to discuss the church in any depth; but there sure are a lot of questions which I would like to have answered.

Exactly what is Metropolitan Community Church?

Is it a Christian church or is it a Gay church?

Who founded the church? and when? and where?

This speaker mentioned that it was an international church. How many countries have churches like this?

How many cities are there in the United States which have a Metropolitan Community Church?

Can you attend the services if you are not homosexual?

Why don't Gay people go to a regular church?

I thought that the Bible said it was a sin to be a homosexual. If that's the case, how can these people have a
Christian church?

How many homosexuals are there in the United States?

How many of them attend religious services at this
church?

Do they allow women to attend, or only men?

Are there any other Gay churches in this country?

Where are they located?

Who ordains these people to be ministers?

Do they ordain women, or just men?

Do they have any publications?

Can you locate the passages in the Bible where it
speaks about homosexuality?

Does the pope know about this church?

III. It sure seems as though the decade of the 1970's has
ushered in a renewed interest in religion in the United States;
and I'm wondering just how that phenomenon came about, and
how long it may last. Every time I turn a corner or sit
down on a bus or something, I always seem to run into a
born-again Christian or one of those Hare Krishna people or
a Jehovah's Witness; and they are more than eager to spend
as much time as possible telling me about their conversion
and how they found the truth or the Lord or something like
that. Anyway, these people really have touched off something
inside of me to find out more about them, but I'm not really
sure what it is I want to know.

I think what I would like to do is begin with a good general
history of religion in the United States, maybe one that could
tell me in a very general way about the earliest religions in
this country. Most of the early religions were imported from
England, weren't they? Or were there already some religions
here when the colonists arrived?

I would also like a history that would go into the beginnings

of some of these strange and foreign religions. Since I do
not really know when they began I really do not know where
to look. Are there any histories of religion that go from the
beginning of religion in the United States to the present day,
and that would cover all of these miscellaneous and fragmented
religious groups?

How many of these odd little religions exist in the
United States today?

Is there any way of finding out exactly how many individuals belong to these groups?

Do most of these religions believe in Jesus or some
other god; or are there some that have no god?

A friend of mine, when I was telling her about some
of the strange people I met, asked me if I had ever heard of
the I Am group. I had not. What are they all about?

Are all of these religions tied in with what is generally known as the "charismatic movement" in the United
States? Was that something started by John Kennedy? I
know people used to always talk about how he had such char-
isma, but I always thought he was Catholic.

And what exactly is "evangelical"? Does that refer
to any specific religion, or is it just a general term that is
used by a lot of different religions?

Is there any way I could locate the address of the
headquarters of some of these groups in the United States,
like the Hare Krishnas or the Children of God? I think that
I might like to write them to get a little more information
about what they believe in; or could I find most of that information here in the library?

I also would need to know what the name of the person
in charge of the church is, and how I should address a letter
to that person.

I was reading something recently about some group
that bought up a whole lot of land in the state of West Virginia; and how they are all very busy building temples and
things like that which will draw a tourist crowd. How could
I find out what the name of the group is? Where would I be
able to locate photographs of what some of their temples look

like? I think I'd also like some information on how the people who live around these various areas are reacting to their
new neighbors.

I imagine that a lot of these small groups have publications that are printed up for people in their own locality,
like newsletters. Do any of them have any publications which
are sent out all over the country? Generally, are these publications free, or do you have to pay for them?

What about missionaries? Do most of these little
groups have their own missionaries who rove about the country trying to convert people to their own religion or group?

Are there any children involved in these little religions,
or is it primarily adults?

Do a lot of these groups have offices in other countries as well, or are most of them just found in this country?

IV. I'm trying to dig up some information on the Bible, because I do not really understand what the origin of it is. I
had always thought that there was just one basic Bible that
everyone used, but that does not seem to be the case. And
I'm not sure whether I want a book or an article, just not
anything too long. What I'd like to know is:

Where was the Bible originally written?

When was the Bible originally written?

Was the Bible written by only one person? If not,
how many different people actually took part in writing it?

Was the Bible written to be a complete work; or was
it written in bits and pieces, and then put together at a later
period in time? When exactly was the first Bible published?

Were there any Bibles published during Jesus' lifetime?

I'm sure that the Bible was not written in English, but
I'd like to know what language it was written in. Whatever
language that is, are there still people around who speak the
language?

If there are not any people who speak that language,

aren't there a lot of problems involved in translating a work that old and that big? After all, how is somebody going to know what the Bible really says?

Are there any books around that do nothing but explain what the Bible says? If not, then how do priests and ministers know what things mean?

Does every religion have its own Bible, or are there some religions that use the same Bible that another religion does?

Do the Jews use a Bible? Do they call it that?

Are there any Bibles that are written in Jewish?

How many foreign languages has the Bible been translated into?

What was the date of the first translation into English?

Do Bibles have to be approved by the church that uses them? Who exactly is the person who grants the approval?

Do a lot of people disagree as to what the Bible says, or to what it means by what it says?

Are all the people who appear in the Bible real, or are some of them just thrown in to make a point?

Is there any place I could look to find pictures of some of the people who do appear in the Bible? Are there any pictures of what the devil looks like?

Where could I find pictures of pages of different Bibles, to see how much of a difference there actually is in how Bibles look?

What is the best-selling Bible in this country?

Do most homes in this country have a Bible?

What is the most expensive Bible that has ever been sold?

If I'm looking to buy a Bible, what should I be looking for? Is there some sort of book that can tell the average person how to evaluate a Bible?

LITERATURE

LITERATURE

Please provide a complete bibliographic citation for at least
one source that will provide an answer to each of the following questions.

1. What is the earliest recorded document of French lit-
    erature?

2. I need a complete list of works by Chaucer.

3. What is the difference between drama and theater?

4. What is the best edition of the collected works of Ben-
    jamin Franklin?

5. How many novels have been written by Barbara Cart-
    land?

6. Who is Judy Blume?

7. Who wrote The Last of the Mohicans?

8. In how many separate novels does Tom Swift appear?

9. When was the sturm und drang period of German lit-
    erature?

10. What were the social ramifications of Goethe's The
    Sorrows of Young Werther?

11. Who were the major French Symbolist poets?

12. Who wrote the world's longest novel?

51

13. Who wrote the world's best novel?

14. Was Death in Venice ever made into a movie? Who wrote the screenplay?

15. What is the etymology of the word Romance?

16. When was the Italian literary Renaissance?

17. When was the Harlem Renaissance?

18. Who are the major authors of Ethiopia?

19. Were Madame Bovary and Flowers of Evil both published in the same year?

20. What is the theme of Silas Marner?

21. Have all of Marcel Proust's works been translated into English?

22. Can you recommend a good anthology of American folk literature, suitable for a teenager?

23. How many critical editions of The Scarlet Letter are in print?

24. What makes a good poem good?

25. Who proposed the theory of the objective correlative? To what does it apply?

26. In 1966, John Flanagan wrote an article entitled "American Literary Bibliography in the Twentieth Century." In what journal did this article appear?

27. How many different editions are there of The Art of Literary Research?

28. What is the best-known work of Brendan Behan?

29. Where could I locate criticism written in the past three years of The Great Gatsby?

30. With which literary genre, and which geographical area, is the name James Branch Cabell associated?

31. Where could I find an intimate biography of William Faulkner?

32. Is Sylvia Plath an American writer?

33. Has Erica Jong received any awards for the works she has written?

34. Did George Sand really devote two hours of every day to writing books?

35. What is the literary significance of Pamela?

36. How many essays did Alexander Pope write?

37. Who was the best French writer of Italian sonnets?

38. Have any writers from South America been awarded the Nobel Prize for Literature?

39. Where could I find a list, with annotations, of stories written about horses?

40. Are there any magazines published in this country which cater to aspiring writers?

41. Who were the most significant writers of closet drama?

42. When was The Well of Loneliness written? When was the first American edition?

43. Who wrote The Autobiography of Alice B. Toklas?

44. Where could I locate articles about nationalism in 19th-century Russian literature?

45. What are the most popular literary games?

46. Can you give me the title of a monthly science fiction magazine?

47. Does semantics play a large role in literary criticism?

48. Do any illustrators of children's books also write books for children?

49. What were the complete names of the Brothers Grimm?

50. Who is the best living contemporary American female poet?

51. What was the name of the optometrist in The Great Gatsby?

52. Were any of Hermann Hesse's novels not published during his lifetime?

53. With which school of poetry is Louise Labé identified?

54. How many short stories did O. Henry write?

55. Has travel literature ever been a popular literary genre in the United States?

56. What is the oldest literary journal in the United States?

57. In addition to the MLA International Bibliography, does the Modern Language Association publish anything?

58. Where did Christopher Isherwood spend most of his life?

59. Is it true that Gustave Flaubert read all of his works aloud to make sure that they sounded right?

60. Is James Baldwin currently working on another novel?

61. During the 1960's, were any of the best-sellers also considered to have important literary significance?

62. Are there any recordings of the poetry of Ezra Pound?

63. Did Shakespeare write all of the plays attributed to him?

64. What is the stated purpose of the Coordinating Council of Literary Magazines? Where could I write them?

65. How much does Playboy magazine pay for articles?

66. Where could I find a review of Trotsky in Exile?

67. Are Knut Hamsun's works considered to be erotic?

68. Where could I locate a good discussion of the style and themes of Henrik Ibsen?

69. How many different authors are being published in the Center for Textual Studies series?

70. Has Edward Albee ever made any statements about the works of Harold Pinter?

71. What is poetic license?

72. Who was F. Scott Fitzgerald's editor?

73. Who currently holds the rights to the works of Willa Cather?

74. Where could I locate information on the politics of Soviet literature?

75. Where could I find some citations and abstracts dealing with morphology?

76. Is Paddy Chayevsky an American or a Russian writer?

77. Where could I locate full bibliographic information on The Oxford Chekhov?

78. Does Studies in Short Fiction review books?

79. How many editions of collected works of Alexandre Dumas have been published?

80. What was Thomas Mann's philosophy of the novel?

81. Are there any good histories of modern Greek literature?

82. Has the Association for the Advancement of Baltic Studies published any monographs?

83. Who is the current chairman or president of the National Council of Teachers of English?

84. Is Rumanian considered to be a Romance language?

85. Are there any good films or filmstrips about Yiddish literature?

86. To what extent did Hassidism influence literature?

87. Where could I locate biographical information about Mario Pei?

88. What is the highest price ever paid for a Faulkner manuscript?

89. What are the major names in Argentine literary criticism?

90. Do any writers today consider the speech to be a literary genre?

91. How frequently is the Romanic Review published?

92. How long has Black Sparrow Press been in existence?

93. What were the major developments in Spanish literature during the past two years?

94. In 1961, Rutgers University Press published a volume of Nigerian folktales. Who were the editors?

95. Are there any collections of African poetry for young readers?

96. Are there any poetic forms that are native to Persia?

97. What did H. L. Mencken think about the quality of American literature?

98. What is the longest play that George Bernard Shaw wrote?

99. Where could I locate a bibliography, preferably annotated, of the literature of Southeast Asia?

100. What are the most popular Eskimo folktales?

101. Where could I find a list of plays that deal with sin?

102. Who was the best author of children's drama?

103. What is the most recent translation of Yukichi Fukuzawa's Autobiography?

104. How many women have won the Pulitzer Prize for poetry?

105. Does Truman Capote think of himself as a regional writer?

106. Were any of the characters in The Scarlet Letter real people?

107. What is a Rabelaisian aesthetic?

108. How many libraries in this country have a complete holding of Poetry?

109. How many articles have been written in English during the past year on the subject of Marcel Proust?

110. What was the first work of Samuel Beckett to achieve critical acclaim?

111. How many different volumes are there of The Diary of Anaïs Nin?

112. Who were the notable American expatriates living in Paris during the first part of this century?

113. What was Ernest Hemingway really like?

114. What is the most valuable Shakespeare folio in the United States?

115. What was the first literary work printed by Gutenberg?

116. Are there any indexes to the letters of Jane Austen?

117. Where could I locate extensive biographical information about Diane Wakoski?

118. Who is Nikki Giovanni's favorite writer?

119. Are there any bibliographies of the works of Gregory Corso?

120. What is the title of a good college-level anthology of 17th-century English literature?

121. Did Jonathan Swift write any books that were not satirical?

122. Are there any collections of criticism of the works of Thomas Hardy?

123. Is Maurice, by E. M. Forster, an autobiographical novel?

124. What is the best critical edition of the poems of Emily Dickinson?

125. What was George Eliot's real name?

126. Are there any annotated editions of The Hunting of the Snark?

127. Who published the most complete edition of Lady Chatterley's Lover?

128. Is William Dean Howells considered a major name in the history of American literature?

129. What exactly was the relationship between Gertrude Stein and Alice B. Toklas?

130. Who is the major biographer of Henry James?

131. Where could I locate imprint information for a book titled Mister Pepys and Mr. Evelyn (1935)?

132. Who owns Paris Review?

133. What is the title and date of publication of the first French Romantic novel?

134. What were the birth and death dates of George Gordon, Lord Byron?

135. In 1967, S. H. Elbert wrote an article entitled "Fate of Poetry in a Disappearing Culture: The Case of Rennell and Bellona in Outer Polynesia." In which journal was this article published?

136. Were any articles about Rumanian fiction published in 1968?

137. I'm trying to locate an essay about André Gide, written by Henri Peyre. It was published sometime during the past five years.

138. Where could I find abstracts of English-language articles that have been published in the past three years, dealing with sex and 20th-century drama?

139. What are the standard French and German dictionaries of poetics?

140. How many computerized data bases exist in the field of literature?

141. I need the titles of three books that are representative of psychological biography as a genre.

142. How many essays have been written during the past year about the essay as a literary genre?

143. Alienación y literatura de protesta, by J. F. Reyes Baena, published in 1972, contained a collection of articles. Where were these articles first published?

144. Which authors are discussed in The Social Novel in England, 1830-1850, by Louis François Cazamian?

145. What was Janet Flanner's pen name?

146. What is the most scholarly monograph about the works of Jean Genet?

147. Are there any atlases of poets and poetry?

148. Approximately how many literary societies are there in the United States?

149. Where could I get a literary guide to Ireland?

150. I need a list of books and articles about how to write drama.

LITERATURE

Search Problems

A.   I would like to locate some information on teaching literature appreciation on the community college level.   I have
been teaching it for a few years now; but each year it seems
to get harder and harder to make my students appreciate what
we are reading.   Maybe part of the problem is in the selections that I have them read.   I'm just not sure.   Is there any
place I can find lists which other teachers might use in their
literature appreciation courses, to see how my lists compare
with those?   Also, I would like to locate some articles, or
abstracts of articles that have come out in the past few years
about teaching literature appreciation on any level.   Has much
been written on this subject?   Since a number of my students
come from varied ethnic backgrounds, I'm wondering if that
could be part of the problem.   Has anything at all been written on the problems of teaching literature appreciation to people who have English as a second language?

B.   As the serials librarian in a four-year liberal arts college library, you are asked by the director to evaluate current titles the library is receiving.   She would also like you
to suggest new titles that might be added in a few areas not
currently covered.   One of these areas is light fiction.   The
memo you receive requests that you supply, with annotations,
a list of the ten periodicals that would be best to supplement
the educational curriculum of the institution, as well as provide light reading for the student body.   In addition to the annotations, you must also rate the periodicals from 1 to 10,
indicating the priority in which they should be received.   How
would you proceed in supplying the information?   Which ten
titles would you list?

C.   I am interested in locating some American literature from
the Colonial period.   Not only do I want to examine some literary writings of the more famous authors, but also general

writers who were influential in their day. I'm afraid that
some of these might not still be available in hard copy, so
I'm wondering if there are any collections of early American
literature which are published in a microformat of any sort.
Where could I find out? Also, I would like to locate some
reviews of these collections, to see if the selection of materials is fairly extensive. Where could I find the reviews?

D. I have to give a twenty-five-minute speech on the development of the short story as a literary genre. It is for my
freshman composition course, so I do not think that the instructor wants it to be too technical or anything. Among the
points that she wants me to cover is what makes a short
story a short story; that is, what the difference is between
a short story and a novella. Is length the only thing that
makes a short story a short story? I have to give examples
as well. And I also have to point out any differences that
might exist between the American short story and the British
short story.

E. I have lots and lots of ideas in my head about different
things that I could write and have published. My problem is
that I really am not sure how good of a writer I am. Once
I decide that, I need to know where to send these items off
to for possible publication. I have been writing a fair amount
of poetry during the past six months, but I have not shown it
to anyone. Where would I take it if I wanted someone to look
at it and tell me how good it is? I also have written some
chapters to a few novels that I keep thinking about. Would
the same type of person be able to read those, and to tell
me whether or not to finish the books? Once I know how
good they are, how do I go about having them published? Are
there certain magazines in this country that publish only poetry? What are their names and addresses? Would it be
possible to find out in advance how much they pay for poems?
Most of the poems are inspirational, if that makes a difference. Would it be better to try to sell my work through an
agent?

F. For a high school English class, my teacher wants each
of us to locate some information about five writers. What
we have to do is find out when they were born; when they died;
how much they wrote; when they wrote it; and why they were
considered important. If they wrote a lot, she said we could
list just their most famous things. We can use any book or
article, except for an encyclopedia, for the information. My
five writers are John Steinbeck, John O'Hara, Pearl Buck,

William Saroyan, and James Baldwin. Where should I go to find the information?

G. For a women's studies course which I am taking, we have to do a ten-page research paper on any aspect of American life which affects women. I thought it might be interesting to do a little study on how marriage as an institution has been described in American literature. I think that maybe the topic is too broad; that I may have to limit it to a particular type of literary genre such as the novel, or drama. Has anyone done any similar studies, which I might use to get some general direction to the paper? Are there any books which might describe various aspects of American life as it appears in literature? Or any subject indexes which I could use to locate some literature which includes the topic of marriage? If possible, I would prefer to use only material which has been written by women. Not the literature itself, but the interpretation of the literature.

H. I have three children between the ages of eight and fourteen; and I'm a little concerned about the type of literature which they are reading in the schools these days. My problem is, I don't know exactly what I want them to read. I just want it to be good. Surely there must be some good literature written for children. You know, something that helps to give them values and make them better people. Are there any lists of good literature for children, lists which might tell me a little bit about the type of book, what age level it is for, and how well written the book is? I especially don't want them reading anything about sex or drugs. Are there any authors who write books for children who also write books for adults?

I. For my humanities class, we have to give a brief talk about a particular poet, and an explication of some of that person's more famous poems. The person I got assigned is Wallace Stevens, and I have no idea where to begin. I have never read anything by him. In fact, I never heard of him until the instructor gave the assignment. What's worse is that I have no idea how to analyze a poem. The instructor said not to worry, that we could find everything we needed at the library. So where do I look? Are there some books which will tell me how to read and analyze a poem? And where am I going to find poetry by this Stevens person? How will I know which poems are the best ones, or which ones I should talk about in class?

J. I'm trying to locate some information on a small poetry press which may or may not still be in existence. The information which I have on it so far is somewhat sketchy. I think it was started sometime in the 1950's by a man named Lawrence Ferlinghetti. It was called City Lights Press. I only heard these names one other time, and that was in relation to Allen Ginsberg; but I have no idea what his relationship was with the other two names. Basically, what I would like to know is the history of this press and exactly what they have published. I think that it may have something to do with the "beat generation," but I'm not even sure what that is.

K. Our local theater group is thinking of adding a period play to our repertoire, and we thought that we would do something which is from the Romantic period. I volunteered to get together a list of possible plays from which we might choose. So to be ready for our next meeting, I need to find out who the major French and German Romantic dramatists were; what were their best plays, and which of these have been translated into English. Since there are only four men in our group, we might have to limit our choice to plays which have no more than four male characters. Also, I will need to draw up an historical note for the playbill, in which I shall have to include some information on the drama of that time period and the playwright that we choose. Where could I find this information?

L. The other day a guest speaker at the Women's Literary Guild was reviewing the last published works of Virginia Woolf and Gertrude Stein. There are a number of questions I have regarding the two--let me see if I can find my notes. Oh yes, first of all ... the name Bloomsbury (or something like that) kept coming up. I'd like to know what that is. Alice P. Toklas is another name I would like to know more about. Can you tell me what, if any, literary relationship existed between Virginia Woolf and Gertrude Stein. I have also been curious about whether either woman was ever married. Where could I find a list of everything that each woman wrote? Finally, have there been any formal studies done which compare the works of Virginia Woolf and Gertrude Stein?

M. I have to hand in a paper in four days for my American lit class, and I don't know where to begin. The professor wants us to do a paper on "The Significance of Theme and Symbolism in Nathaniel Hawthorne's Scarlet Letter." Since

I have not even read the book, I need to know what it is
about, and to locate as much information as I can relative
to the topic.

N. My brother is a real science fiction nut, and seems to
read just about everything that is published. You should see
his bedroom. He must have about five hundred paperbacks
just thrown all over the place. Well, his birthday is coming
up, and I thought it might be nice if I bought him some sort
of encyclopedia of science fiction or some sort of reference
book like that. I never read the stuff myself, so I really
don't know what kind of books there are that he might like.
Do you have any lists here at the library? I would really
like to find something for under twenty-five dollars if possible. Since he is going to be twenty-two, he probably is
able to read almost anything. What would you recommend?

O. For an American studies seminar, our instructor wants
us to type up a bibliography of articles and books, written in
any language, on a particular topic which he assigned. My
topic is "Color Symbolism in the Works of Herman Melville."
He said that he wants the bibliography to be as exhaustive as
possible, but that it should cover material which was published
from 1935 to 1975. How many different places am I going to
have to look to make sure that I do not overlook any item
which was published during that time? Are there any bibliographies of Melville's works which might help?

P. Being a music buff, I have been struck by the nationalism
which is so predominant in some of the works of 19th-century
Russian composers. I'm wondering how common nationalism
was in the literature of the same time period; that is, did
many of Russia's great writers from that time period try to
incorporate nationalism into their works? If they did, is
there any way of finding out to what extent the literature influenced the music, and vice versa? Who were the major
Russian writers of that time period?

Q. For a bibliography course which I am taking, our instructor wants us to take two writers and compare translations of
their works, supposedly to get at the problems involved in
translating literature. Personally, I think it is a waste of
time, but the project is due in three weeks. What we have
to do is choose one ancient author and one modern foreign
author. I have chosen Aristophanes and Françoise Sagan.
Now I have to find out how many of their works have been
translated into English within the past twenty years; and to

locate reviews of those translations, paying particular attention to how much of the review actually discusses the quality
of the translation. Where can I go to find the information I
need? I'll sure be glad when this semester is over.

R. I would like to find some information about some of the
kings and knights and queens and ladies that appear in a lot
of medieval writing. People like King Arthur and the Knights
of the Round Table; and Guinevere, and Robin Hood and Maid
Marion. Were these people real people? I mean, did they
actually live? And did they do all those things that people
have written about? Is there any way to find out what was
the first book that they were mentioned in? I have noticed
that their names come up a lot in Romantic literature, but
I wonder if people from other time periods wrote about them.
Is there any way to find out, for instance, in how many novels King Arthur and Queen Guinevere appear? Or whether
all those novels were in the English language?

S. Do you have any books here in the library that would tell
me a little something about American Indian literature? What
I want to know is who the major Indian writers were, and are,
in this country? Did they all pretty much come from the
same tribes, or did every tribe have some good writers?
What was the general status of literature in Indian culture?
What I mean by that is, exactly how important was literature
to the average Indian? And what kind of literature was it?
What kinds of subjects did Indians write about?

T. My English instructor keeps talking about the importance
of literary criticism in the field of literature. She says that
in order to understand the development of literature, it is
necessary to understand the development of criticism because
it is criticism that makes or breaks an author. Is that true?
How important has criticism been to the development of literature? Has anybody written about this subject? Or are there
any general histories of literary criticism? Is there any way
I could find out, for example, who the major literary critics
of the past two centuries were?

LITERATURE

Case Studies

I.   I just returned from a day of junking, during which I
bought a little paperback edition of a play which was written
by Isla Paschal Richardson.   Much to my surprise, there was
a letter written by the author inside of the book.   The letter
itself is very fascinating because part of it is typed, while
part of it is written in Miss Richardson's own hand.   Dated
February 19, 1935, it is addressed to a Mrs. Dalton, who
apparently was living in Nashville, Tennessee, at the time.   The
return address is Tullahoma, Tennessee; and the letterhead reads

Nashville Branch
of the
National League of American Pen Women
Incorporated

and goes on to list the following officers: Clyde Burke Mill-
spaugh, President; Maude McGehee Hankins, Vice-President;
Margaret Lindsley Warden, Sec.-Treas.; Florence A. Wilson,
Registrar; and Clara Cox Epperson, Auditor.

I am very excited about the purchase because the letter may
be an item of some value, or at least may be of help to
someone who is studying about the author.   But I really do
not know anything about Isla Paschal Richardson, except that
she wrote the book that I bought.   She does mention a few of
her other plays in her letter to Mrs. Dalton, but I really
would like more information about the people, the organization, and the plays.   Where can I look to find answers to
these questions:

Who was Isla Paschal Richardson?   When was she
born and is she still alive?

Did she marry anyone important?   or did she come
from some prominent Tennessee family?

66

How many plays did she write in her lifetime?

Did she do anything else, other than writing plays?

How important of a writer was she?

Were her plays very popular? Where were they presented or performed?

Who is Mrs. Dalton? Did she ever write anything? The book I bought has a name penciled in at the top which seems to read "May Herbert-Dalton." Is that her? Which name did she go by?

Who are those other people who are listed as officers of this group? Are they all writers, too?

What was, or is, the National League of American Penwomen?

Did they only write plays, or maybe some novels, too?

How many chapters did they have nationwide? Is there any way I could find out if they still exist?

The book which I bought is The Cancelled Debt, published by the Walter H. Baker Company of Boston in 1934. At the top of the title page are the words "National League of Penwomen Plays." Was this a series? If so, how many plays were published as part of the series?

How could I find out if there are any special collections which have the plays or letters of Miss Richardson?

Is it allright for me to make a copy of the letter, or is that illegal?

Where would I be able to find out if either the letter or the book itself has any significant monetary value?

Miss Richardson also mentions a group called the Twentieth Century Club. Could you find out where they were located, and whether or not it was a writer's group?

II. For an Afro-American studies course, we have to do a twenty-five-page research paper about some aspect of Afro-

American culture. I'm not sure which topic I want to write about, but I would like it to be in the area of literature. Before I decide, I want to get more information regarding certain aspects.

Who was the first Black person to achieve any sort of literary fame in the United States? What was their most important work? Were they born in America or in another country?

If I wanted to buy the ten best Black novels ever written, where could I find out what they were?

Have any non-Blacks been praised for their accurate portrayal of the Black experience in America?

I've heard the name of Nikki Giovanni a few times. I think that she's a poet who has had a fair amount of her work published. Are there many reviews of her collection of poetry? When did she first start writing? What is her status among other Black poets?

Where could I find information on the history of Black publishing? What I'd like to know is whether or not most Black writers have had a hard time getting published by mainstream publishers.

What was the first Black-owned publishing enterprise in this country? What kinds of material did it publish? Is the publishing house still in operation today?

What about James Baldwin? Is he considered to be a very important writer of the 20th century? What were his roots; and how did he get his start in writing?

Has anyone done any studies about the extent to which Black American literature reflects both African and American values? Are those values basically the same?

Which of the notable Black African authors has been most widely read by Black Americans? Do Black authors in this country feel that their work is heavily influenced by their African ancestors?

In general, it seems that women have always received less literary attention than men. Is that also true in the area of Black literature?

In some of the reading I have done, I have come across the name Harlem Renaissance. I'm not sure, but I think it may have been a particular school of Black literature. Where could I find out more about what the term referred to?

Who were the most significant authors of the Harlem Renaissance? Did it include more than authors? Are any of the authors still alive today?

Are there any literary series which contain only Black authors?

I also want to know a little about the developments of Black drama in the United States. Most of the plays I've read in American literature courses always had Black characters in minor roles which were not very flattering. Prior to 1950, were there any plays written in the country which had Blacks in major roles? Not only major roles, but roles which were dignified and non-stereotyped?

Are there many Black dramatists writing today? What about Black women? How many of them are writing plays?

Have any Black American authors been honored with any national or international literary prizes?

III. For a project we all have to do for our comparative literature course, our instructor wants us to take any foreign country and report on the major authors (no more than fifteen) of literary significance. He said that most of them should still be living, but we could pick a few authors who are dead. What we have to do is give basic information about each author, including birth and death dates; city of birth; formal education; any additional education or experience which helped them as a writer; as complete a list of their publications as we can find; any separately published criticisms of their works. As if that were not enough, we then have to supplement this with a five-page statement which talks about the relative status of each author compared to the others. And we also have to indicate trends or general characteristics of the national literature which these authors display.

For my project, I chose Canada. I have a list with some names already, but I'll need to find some book or something that talks about Canadian authors in general. The names I have are: Ann Blades, Margaret Atwood, Pierre Burton,

Joyce Carol Oates, Margaret Lawrence, Mordecai Richler, Michel Tremblay, Lucy Maud Montgomery, Hugh McLennan, Gabrielle Roy, and Marie-Claire Blais.

Except for Joyce Carol Oates, I have not read anything by any of these authors. How am I going to find out which of them is living and which of them is dead?

I will also need to find out whether they all write in English, or whether some of them write in French.

Do they all write just novels, or do some of them write in other genres? I have read some poems by Joyce Carol Oates; but I just don't know about the others.

Is there any way that I could find out if any of them is currently working on another novel or something, and when they expect that work to be published?

Are there any good histories of Canadian literature? Are there any good histories that cover only the 20th century?

Because Canada is bilingual, I think it is important to include authors from both the English and French cultures. But at the same time, I would like my selection to represent the reality of things. How would I go about finding out whether there are more authors writing in English or in French, as well as how the average Canadian feels about literature written in both languages?

One trend in the literature that I have noticed already is that there seem to be more female than male writers in Canada. Is this actually true? Is there any place I could locate any explanation of this?

I would also like to locate some stuff about how Canadian literature is viewed on an international level. I mean, do writers in other countries take Canadian writers seriously? It seems that here in the United States, no one seems to know a whole lot about Canadian literature. In fact, they don't seem to know a whole lot about Canada in general.

Well ... any help you can give me to get me started on the project would be appreciated.

IV. I've always been a big fan of cowboy movies and general

Westerns, but only recently have I started reading Westerns. It is like a whole new world has opened up. Some of the books are pretty much like the movies which I have seen; but some of them are completely different, presenting pictures of the Old West that I guess are more realistic, or at least describe things more like they really were back then. I am a little puzzled about how there could be such different images of the same subject. Anyway, I also seem to have discovered a whole new area of reading, and I really would like to start reading more novels about the Old West, preferably those that have some sort of accuracy to them. My problem is that I don't know where to look. Some of the stuff I read as a kid, but I really don't remember who the authors were; and being a kid, I wasn't all that concerned about the accuracy, just the adventure.

Does the library have any kind of list of cowboy novels or novels that take place in the Old West? I'm not even sure what I mean when I say that. When exactly was the Old West? Are there dates that everybody agrees upon?

Were there a lot of people writing novels about the Old West during that time period? I think it might be interesting to get a hold of some of those books, just to see if people today write about it in the same way as the people who wrote about it back then.

Is there a difference between a cowboy novel and a Western? Have there been any written which were considered to be great literature?

Are Westerns or cowboy novels or whatever read by a lot of people in this country? How do they compare with other subjects that people read about, in terms of sales?

Do any publishers have complete series of Western novels? Or are there any publishers who publish nothing but this type of literature?

Are Westerns considered to be regional literature? What I mean is, did most of the authors who wrote this stuff actually live in the West; or are some of them the type that lived in New York City all their lives and never saw a cowboy or a cow?

Who is the most popular Western writer?

Which writer of novels about the Old West has written the most novels, or at least published the most novels?

Do most public libraries have pretty big collections of Western literature? Are they all pretty much the same; or do you think if I couldn't find a book here that I might be able to find it at one of the nearby public libraries?

I would kind of like to get my sons interested in reading some of this stuff, too. I think it would help to pull their faces away from the front of the television; and I think they might like some of the adventure that goes on in a lot of these books. My problem there is that I don't think they would be able to read all of the same stuff that I read. Again, do you have any list of cowboy novels for children or teenagers? One of them is nine; the other is twelve.

In addition to any lists you might have, for me or the kids, is there anything here that would not only list the books, but also tell a little bit about them, and maybe even say whether they are worth reading or not?

Is it very hard to get a hold of some of the older novels? Do most libraries own them, or am I going to have a hard time trying to find them?

MUSIC

MUSIC

Questions

Please provide a complete bibliographic citation for at least one source that will provide an answer to each of the following questions.

1. How many songs has Nina Simone written?

2. Who is Sun Ra?

3. Do all pianos have eighty-eight keys?

4. How many octaves are there?

5. Who is credited with having invented the modern method of musical notation?

6. What is the vocal range of a basso profundo voice?

7. How many composers with the surname Bach have there been?

8. Where could I locate the musical score to Hair?

9. Has anything been written about Zulu music during the past ten years?

10. What are the most popular folk instruments in Peru?

11. Are there any cultures that have no instrumental music?

12. What other composers did Beethoven know during his lifetime?

13. How many people are there in a symphony orchestra?

14. Who invented the violin?

15. What is the difference between a violin and a viola?

16. Which of Stockhausen's works is the most celebrated?

17. Has John Cage written anything about his philosophy of music?

18. Is there a difference between a theme and a melody?

19. What are the most popular religious hymns in this country?

20. How many versions of "The Star-Spangled Banner" are there?

21. Where did Van Cliburn make his musical debut?

22. Why are so many musical directions written in Italian?

23. Who wrote the longest symphony?

24. Where could I find some pictures of Renaissance instruments?

25. How popular was vocal music in 18th-century France?

26. What was the name of the man who compiled the definitive catalog of Mozart's music?

27. Why are tubas so big?

28. How much formal study does a conductor need?

29. How many people does the Metropolitan Opera House seat?

30. What was the first recorded opera in which Maria Callas appeared?

31. What contribution did Jelly Roll Morton make to music?

32. Where could I locate a critical review of Stevie Wonder's latest album?

33. Did Haydn write any music for flute?

34. What is the theme of The Jupiter Symphony?

35. What does a devil's fiddle look like?

36. How many albums has Joan Baez recorded?

37. Can you recommend a good history of urban blues music?

38. Who were the most important composers of the Middle Ages?

39. Who invented the Moog synthesizer?

40. What is Dolly Parton's real name?

41. How much does Chuck Mangione charge for a concert performance?

42. How many English-language operas are there?

43. What are the most appropriate musical pieces to play at a wedding?

44. What is the difference between a first-chair and a second-chair performer in an orchestra?

45. How many people do you need to have a marching band?

46. What are the general characteristics of Baroque music?

47. How many recorded collections of Beethoven's symphonies are currently available for purchase?

48. To whom could I sell a few songs that I have written?

49. Can you recommend a good collection of Christmas carols?

50. Who wrote the music and lyrics for Showboat?

51. Where could I locate some information on the Kentucky Opera Association?

52. What is the name of B. B. King's latest album?

53. Where is the Interlochen Music Academy?

54. In 1978, C. Schwandt wrote an article about Eliahu Inbal. What was the title of the article, and where was it published?

55. Has Chick Corea written any articles? About what?

56. Are there any musical festivals in Luxembourg?

57. Is Dietrich Fischer-Dieskau still alive?

58. Has Benjamin Britten written any choral music?

59. Is Barry Brown considered an important name in country music?

60. In 1977, Henry Bruinsma delivered a speech to the National Federation of Music Clubs Annual Board Meeting. What was the title of the speech? Was it ever published?

61. Did any music magazines review The Destroyer: Acid Rock, by R. Sapir and W. Murphy?

62. Who is the author of Electronic Music: Systems, Techniques, and Controls?

63. Who was the translator of Wagner Writes from Paris: Stories, Essays and Articles by the Young Composer?

64. What were the top pop records in 1970?

65. Has anyone done any critical studies of Bach organ music?

66. Where could I locate a review of Purcell's Jubilate Deo in D; for trumpets, strings, organ and voices, arranged by W. Shaw?

67. In 1956, I. Parrott authored an article on experimental music. What was the title? Where was it published?

68. How many articles were written in 1954 concerned with ethnomusicology?

69. Does the American Guild of Organists still give choir master examinations?

70. Where could I find some harp songs from Uganda?

71. How many colleges and universities in the Southeast offer performance degrees?

72. How many madrigal societies are there in the United States?

73. Is Tom T. Hall a member of ASCAP?

74. How much will a union musician be paid in New York City?

75. Has the Music Publishers Association of the United States issued any statements on copyright?

76. How many recorded versions are there of My Fair Lady?

77. Can you recommend a good one-volume work on opera management?

78. Who were the members of the Original Dixieland Jazz Band?

79. What sort of equipment is necessary to tune a piano?

80. Can you give me the names of some companies that manufacture banjo strings?

81. What company owns the rights to Cole Porter's music?

82. Does a discography generally tell you the same thing a bibliography does?

83. Who was the most popular jazz saxophonist in 1964?

84. How much does it cost to produce one copy of one long-playing album?

85. What are some good examples of Gypsy music?

86. Who owns Downbeat magazine?

87. How many histories of music has Curt Sachs written?

88. What is the best French dictionary of music?

89. Is there a French Academy of Music? How does one become a member?

90. Where is the Country Music Hall of Fame?

91. How extensive were Elvis Presley's property holdings when he died?

92. Do they allow jazz in Russia?

93. What sort of requirements are there to be a music teacher?

94. Why did Dionne Warwick sue Burt Bacharach for $6,000,000?

95. Has much been written about English theater music in the 18th century?

96. How can you tell if an auditorium has good acoustics?

97. How many computerized data bases exist in the field of music?

98. Has the U.S. Government published any musical scores?

99. Did Berlioz ever write anything about Beethoven?

100. Where could I locate biographical information on Charles Ives?

101. What techniques are used for dating early published music?

102. How frequently is the Tennessee Folklore Society Bulletin published?

103. Where are the corporate headquarters of ABC Records?

104. Can you recommend a good book to teach me guitar?

105. What is the name of the person who developed playing the inside of a piano?

106. How many reeds does an accordion have?

107. What is the difference between a French horn and a coronet?

108. What is Shostakovich's best work?

109. By what popular name is Belle Silverman known?

110. Where are the headquarters of the Music Library Association?

111. Where could I locate an extensive biography of Liberace, along with a few photographs?

112. What is the title of Gloria Gaynor's most recent recording?

113. Who is the best male tenor alive today?

114. Who is the author of Puissances du jazz (1953)?

115. Who is the publisher of Billboard?

116. Who are the major distributors of foreign sheet music in the United States?

117. Do minstrels still exist?

118. Which three thematic catalogs would be the best ones to have as part of a general music collection?

119. To what does the term "acid rock" refer?

120. Are Ferrante and Teicher related?

121. Did Giselle Mackenzie ever have any best-selling records?

122. How much was Bing Crosby's estate worth when he died?

123. How did Lawrence Welk discover the Lennon Sisters?

124. Was Joni Mitchell ever married? To whom?

125. Have any reviews of Bette Midler's music appeared in Catholic magazines?

126. How many volumes are there in The Oxford History of Music?

127. Is there really a hymn titled "Ain't No Flies on My Lord Jesus"? Who wrote it?

128. How many operas does the Metropolitan Opera Company usually stage during a regular season?

129. Where could I locate critical opinions of Burl Ives' career?

130. What was Dinah Shore's theme song?

131. Who accredits music schools?

MUSIC

Search Problems

A.   My humanities instructor wants us to do a seven-page
paper comparing any two symphonic works, as long as they
are by two different composers.   What we have to do is to
compare how each composer has adapted the symphonic form
to his particular work.   He said that we could also rely on
what different critics have said about each symphony.   My
problem is that even after listening to my instructor talk
about different symphonies in class, I'm not real sure that
I understand what one is.   Where could I find a real good
definition or explanation of a symphony?   I think I want to
compare Beethoven and Brahms; but as for which symphony,
my final choice is going to depend upon how much criticism
I can find about individual symphonies.   I know that Beethoven
did nine symphonies, but how many did Brahms do?   How can
I find out which symphonies have had the most written about
them?

B.   I have been listening to rock music now for close to
fifteen years.   I really do know a lot about the music, and
the major musicians and performers.   But what I don't know
much about is the rock business.   When did rock and roll
first become a major business in this country?   Did it create
a lot of new recording companies, or did the old companies
just add it to their business?   Is there a lot of money to be
made in the business?   I don't mean by the performers, but
by all the people that you never see--like agents, road man-
agers, and even the road crews?   How much money is an
agent likely to make in one year?   And what about record
production?   How much does it usually cost to produce a
record album today?   How many copies of an album does a
company have to sell in order to break even?

C.   Why is chamber music called chamber music?   Is it a
particular kind of music?   I guess I always think of it as

mostly short musical pieces that are written for three or
maybe four instruments at the most. Is there any chamber
music that is written for a large number of instruments?
What are the most frequently used instruments in chamber
music? Has this changed over time, or has it pretty much
stayed the same? Do a lot of living composers still write
chamber music much? Can you give me the names of some
groups that are well known, and that perform the music well?

D. The humanities department at the community college
where I teach is going to begin offering one course in music
history and music appreciation next year, and it has pretty
well been decided that I am the one who is going to teach it.
My training in music is somewhat adequate, but I've always
had a difficult time explaining to people who know nothing
about music exactly what it is that makes some music good
and some music bad. Does the library here have any materials that might help me in preparing the course? I know
which composers and which pieces I would like people to listen to, but it would help if I could locate some explanations
of what to listen for in the music. I would also like to get
a list of some music-history and music-appreciation textbooks
which might be written on a community college student level.

E. It sure seems like disco is one of the big musical fads
of the seventies, but nobody really seems to know anything
about it other than the tunes. How did the disco craze get
started in this country? Did it even start in this country?
Is there any live disco music? Who are the best-selling
performers of disco? Can disco be traced directly to any
other musical form? Is there any sort of philosophy behind
disco music? Is it likely that disco will be as popular in the
eighties as it was in the seventies?

F. For a library science course I am taking, dealing with
problems of cataloging special materials, we all have to do
a brief paper about problems of cataloging some sort of special material. My instructor assigned music and musical recordings to me. I guess I just do not understand why there
is a problem cataloging material like music or musical recordings. Wouldn't you just catalog them the way you would
any other thing? Anyway, where could I find information
about problems in cataloging music? Is it only a concern of
librarians, or are other people interested in this subject?
Has anyone in the field of music written about this problem?

G. What exactly is jazz? It seems like one of those terms

that everybody uses to refer to different things. Are there
a lot of different types of jazz, or is all jazz basically the
same? The only jazz names I know are people like Duke
Ellington and Count Basie. Are there a lot more famous
names in jazz? Is jazz primarily Black music, or are there
some Whites playing jazz? When exactly did jazz get started,
and where? Do most of the major record companies in this
country issue jazz recordings?

H. As the serials librarian in a four-year liberal arts college library, you are asked by the director to evaluate current titles the library is receiving. She would also like you
to suggest new titles that might be added in a few areas not
currently covered. One of these areas is music. The memo
you receive requests that you supply, with annotations, a list
of ten periodical titles that would be best to supplement the
educational curriculum of the institution, as well as provide
light reading for the student body. Currently, the curriculum
contains only two music-appreciation courses, and those are
in the humanities department. In addition to the annotations,
you must also rate the periodicals from 1 to 10, indicating
the priority in which they should be received. How would
you proceed in supplying the information? Which ten titles
would you list?

I. I am really good at working with wood; and I have built
an awful lot of things from scratch. Since my son's birthday
is coming up in about five months, I thought it would be a
nice surprise if I gave him a custom-made guitar which was
made by his father. He is already showing some interest in
music. Looking at the guitars in stores, it doesn't seem as
though they would be that hard to make. Are there any books
or magazines that would show me how to make a guitar? Not
only how to make it, but any special tools which I would need?
And how much it would cost to make?

J. I really do not know a whole lot about Oriental music,
but I want to expand my record collection a bit, to include
at least some representative types of Oriental music. Who
are the major composers of Oriental music who are living
today? Is a lot of the music traditional, or are there some
experimental forms of music? Do any recording companies
in this country record Oriental music, or am I going to have
to buy imported albums? Would the import albums have the
same good technical quality that American albums have?

K. For a class report for her popular music course at

Careen Community College, Janet Anderson has chosen to do
a brief history of musical styles in the United States since
World War II. She has chosen three styles: urban blues,
reggae, and disco. For each of these styles, she is to report on 1) the history of that style since World War II; 2)
the development of that style into other musical styles during
the time period involved; 3) indication of major composers,
arrangers, and performers within the United States; 4) citation of at least five titles for musical style that are representative of that style; and 5) the current status or popularity
of that style within the mainstream of popular music in the
United States today. How would you advise Janet in her pur-
suit of the desired information? Since she has never given
a citation for a recording before, she will need that information as well.

L. Marge Cunningham, a ninth-grade student in Miss Kli-
maxe's music course, has to do a short paper listing ten
musical terms that pertain to the instrument she plays--the
violin. She must also provide the definitions to these terms.
In addition, she must list the name, with birth and death
dates, of at least ten composers who have written music for
the violin. She can get extra credit if she lists two works
by each composer. However, she cannot use any standard
encyclopedia or dictionary for the project. How would you
go about helping Marge?

M. When I was younger my mother used to take me to the
movies a lot. We went to all kinds of movies, but there
were a few which she insisted that we should never miss.
Among those were many movies which had Deanna Durbin and
José Iturbi in major or minor roles. I don't remember a
whole lot about the plots of these movies. All I really remember is that the acting never really struck me as dynamic.
Deanna Durbin would always be singing; and José Iturbi used
to play violin. Well, obviously neither one of them ever made
it big as a superstar or anything, but I'm curious as to exactly what did happen to them after they made those movies.
Where are they now, and what are they doing? They certainly were entertaining, but I wonder how the critics of the
time reacted to them. Is there some way I could find out?
Also, did either of them ever make any recordings which are
still available for purchase?

N. In a year or so, I'm going to be graduating from high
school, and I really would like to go on to college somewhere
and major in music. My music teacher says that that would

probably be a good idea, since I do have a good voice and I am interested in the history-type things in music. She has recommended a few places on the West coast, but I think I would prefer somewhere in the Southeast. Where could I find some information on music programs in the Southeast? I would prefer some place that gave a B.F.A. degree in music, rather than a B.A. degree. I would also like to find a department that had a lot of diversity, and good teachers. How could I find out about that?

O. I am very interested in the computer applications of music composition, but I really do not know where to go to find out more about it. I remember reading something once about someone who fed some of Bach's music into a computer and got a design for a rug which was based on the music. It sounds strange, but interesting. Can you tell me whether that story is true? I would also like to know what is currently being done with music and computers. Are computers writing a lot of the music that is being produced today? Can computers even write music? Are there any composers that are working almost exclusively with a computer rather than more traditional instruments?

P. Back in the sixties, it seemed like there were a lot of counter-culture or alternative magazines being published; and a lot of the titles had a heavy emphasis on music. Since I haven't seen too many of these anymore, I was wondering just how many music magazines of a counter-culture nature are still being published. I don't really remember any specific titles, except for Rolling Stone; but I don't think that that magazine has the same kind of articles that it used to. Does the library have any sort of list of those old sixties music newspapers and magazines? Are there any libraries near here that might even have copies of them? And how could I find out whether they are still being published?

Q. I am interested in finding out what, if anything, is being done in the field of music therapy. Has anyone, particularly musicians, written anything about what sort of applications can be made with music to the therapeutic setting? Is any music therapy being done by musicians rather than by professional psychologists or psychiatrists? I would also like to know if there are any musical recordings which have been made expressly for therapeutic use. Who are the most important people writing in this field today?

R. For one of my high school classes, I have to give a

report about Indians. I talked about the report with my teacher, and she said that I could go ahead and do mine on music and musical instruments of American Indians. She said she wasn't sure how much material I could find, but that it sounded interesting. So where do I go to get some books and magazines and pictures about the music that Indians played? She said we could use anything but an encyclopedia; and I would really like to find lots and lots of pictures, especially of Indians playing their instruments. Are there any records of Indian music? Would you have any here in the library?

S. I would like to know what kind of music was popular among Blacks in the United States during the 18th century. Since most of the Blacks who were in this country then probably still had close African roots, I imagine that a lot of the music was not American at all, but African. Is that right? Has much been written about this subject at all? I would really like to know what kinds of religious music and hymns, if any, were played and sung by Blacks during that time period. Also, things like work songs and chanties--is there any idea of what the most popular songs were, and how they even developed in the first place? Was Black music very sophisticated during that time period?

T. I want to find out something about the history of musical instruments, but I don't really want to read a whole lot about them. What I'm interested in is locating pictures of different musical instruments since the time they were invented to the present. The three instruments I am particularly interested in are the harp, the guitar, and the harmonica. Where could I find out where they were first invented, and who invented them? I would also like to know how many different kinds of harp, guitar, and harmonica there are. Are there any museums that collect musical instruments like these? I thought that maybe I could write them for a copy of their catalog. Would you be able to give me their addresses?

MUSIC

Case Studies

I. For a popular music course that I'm taking over at the local community college, our instructor is having each of us do a thirty-minute speech about some trend in popular music. What we have to do is to give a brief history of that trend (maybe about ten minutes), and then spend the rest of the time playing some musical selections that are examples of that type of music, from the time that it first started up until the present.

The trend that I have decided to do my speech on is rock. I know it is a pretty big area; and I do know a little something about rock in general.   But for this report I am going to have to find out how many different types of rock there are.   You know, things like just plain old rock and roll. Then there's acid rock; and folk rock; and jazz rock; rockabilly; and I'm sure there have to be at least a dozen others.

Where could I go to find a good general history of rock from whenever it first started up to the present time? I also want to find out a little about the origins of the terms themselves.   For instance, who coined the phrase "rock and roll" originally?   Why was the music called that instead of something else?

Was rock and roll the original rock music, or was there rock music around that developed into rock and roll?

Whose names are associated with the beginnings of rock and roll?   I know people like Elvis Presley and Buddy Holly and Fats Domino and the Big Bopper.   But I don't know if these people were all the originators of rock and roll, or if they came along after it got started by somebody else.   Do you think that that might be talked about in some history of music?

One thing that would probably help a lot, if I could find them, are some of the teen magazines from the fifties and sixties, and even the seventies, especially those that gave a lot of coverage to rock stars. My problem there is that I have no idea of what the magazines were called. Where could I find that out?

And once I find out what they were called, how am I going to get a hold of some of the back issues? They certainly don't seem like the type of magazine that most libraries would have. Do you think that this library ever subscribed to them? or even any other library that is nearby?

I think that it might be good to find out who were the best-selling singers of rock, too. Is that the type of thing that would be in a history book? And if it is not there, where else could I look? Oh, I remember there is some magazine called Billboard, which I've seen a few of my friends reading. Maybe that would have it? But how long has Billboard been around?

Since I will only have about twenty minutes to play different albums for the class, I really am going to have to work at which music to select for them to hear. How do you think I could get a list of maybe the best rock songs that were ever recorded? Or instead of doing the best, do you think that I should do the most popular ones? But in twenty minutes I don't think that I could play more than ten. Can you help me decide which ten I should play?

II. I'm trying to dig up some information on Black music in this country, especially Black recording companies. I have looked in a few places already, but I don't seem to be able to find a whole lot of what I'm looking for. The names I have so far are Motown, Blue Note, Tamla and AAMOA Records. I'm kind of familiar with Motown, mainly because of the Supremes, but I still can't find everything I want to know about Black recording companies.

Was Motown the first Black recording company in this country, or were there other companies during the thirties and forties?

What was the first recording ever made by a Black singer? Was it recorded by a Black recording company?

When exactly was Motown Records founded, and where?

The man who used to own it is called Barry Gordie, or Gordy--I'm not sure how it's spelled. Was he also the founder of Motown, or did somebody else do that?

Before the Supremes came along, who was the major individual or group that recorded for Motown? Are they still recording?

Is there any way of finding out how much money was made just from the sale of recordings by the Supremes?

I would also like to find out who the other major artists for Motown were during the sixties and seventies.

Who owns Motown Records now, and where are its headquarters and major recording studios? Is it still producing and selling as many albums as it once did?

What about these other companies? Blue Note, for instance. I think that most of their recordings might be jazz, but I want to know if they record people other than jazz artists. Does Motown record jazz, too?

Who are the major recording artists for Blue Note?

Where is Blue Note located? And who owns that company? How many years has that company been in existence? Is there any way that I could get a complete list of everything that has been recorded by Blue Note?

Does Blue Note have, or has it ever had, any financial connections with Motown or with any other Black recording companies?

And what about these other two recording companies-- Tamla and AAMOA Records. I came across their names in an article I was reading about Black music; but all it did was mention the name, and said nothing else. Are they new recording companies, or have they been around as long as Motown and Blue Note?

Where could I find out where they are located and who owns them?

I would also like to find out who has recorded for them. Where could I find that out?

Is there any way to find out how many albums some

of these companies have sold, so I can compare them to Motown?

There have to be more than just four Black recording companies in this country, don't there? Are there a lot of small companies around, or are there really only four?

Finally, I'd like to know which Black singers--male, female, and group--have sold the most albums to date.

III. Our church auxiliary, along with some other local groups, has decided to plan a three-day Appalachian Heritage Festival for some time next spring. We had our first meeting last week; and since I'm the singer for our church (and the only one at the meeting who knew anything about music), they asked me if I would handle the music part of the festival. Well, what could I do? Of course I said yes, not realizing how much needed to be done. I've got a few notes here from the meeting, mainly about different things that everyone wanted to make sure were included; but I think that this is only the beginning. By the time this is over, I may wish that I never learned to sing.

Since the festival is going to be planned as a general family affair, we want to make sure that the booths and exhibits are eye-catching and educational for the children. In order to do that, we thought that we would have photographs of folk instruments, as well as playing recorded folk music from the Appalachian area. That's my first problem. I don't know anything about Appalachian folk instruments. Well, I shouldn't say I don't know anything. I know the names of a few instruments. But only a few. What I would like to do is to find some sort of listing of folk instruments that were used to play Appalachian music. Either that, or some sort of general history of music. That should mention all of the instruments, shouldn't it?

One thing I really need to find out is which of the instruments was actually invented or created in Appalachia, and which of them came from England or Ireland or wherever when our ancestors came over here.

And, of course, in addition to finding out what the instruments were, and a little bit of history about them, I am also going to need to locate some illustrations which I could photocopy or have reproduced and enlarged by a photographer.

Now, the recordings. I have to locate a list, I guess, of some recordings of Appalachian folk music played on authentic instruments. Do you think that you have a list like that here? Are there a lot of recordings that I could choose from? I really want to find some music that is representative--not just of music that is played today, but from all time.

I imagine that it might be nice, too, if I could find some instruments or copies of instruments to have on display. Do you have any idea of how I would go about locating some? Are there any museums that have collections of folk instruments? Do you think that they might be willing to loan a few for a festival like ours?

You know, it might even be nice if we could locate a few authentic Appalachian folksingers or musicians who could play some music live. I'm sure the children would be interested in seeing some of that. But how do you go about finding these people?

We also thought that, for educational purposes, it would be nice to make up a list of books and records for kids and adults alike. We don't want it to be too long. Maybe about twenty titles which they could get here at the library. Do you think that you have that many books here that would be good enough to put on a list like that?

What about recordings which people could get from here or from a record store?

And we thought it might be nice to include the names of a few organizations which people could write to if they wanted more information about this kind of music. Which ones would you suggest?

IV. I just finished taking a survey of Western music course here that was offered through the Free University; and the person who taught it got me real interested in what's happening with avant-garde music. She only spent about an hour talking about this kind of music, but it was enough to get me to come down here to find out a little more about it.

I remember her saying that it was real hard to give a good definition of what avant-garde music is; or at least she found it real hard to do. Where could I look to find somebody's definition of the term? Or are there a lot of different definitions?

It is probably too recent for anybody to have written a history of this sort of music, but I would like to know exactly when avant-garde music got started. Was there any avant-garde music during the 19th century? If so, who wrote it?

Some of the people involved with avant-garde music seem like they must be real interesting, judging from the type of music that they are composing and producing. Is there any way that I could find out if any of them has written anything about their personal philosophy of music, like what they think good music should be? Or how they think good music should sound?

It might be interesting too, to find out what they think of composers who lived before they did, and the type of music that existed before avant-garde music. Would that be easy to find?

I asked my instructor if she knew of any avant-garde vocal music. She said that she thought there were a few things written for voice, but that she had never heard any of them. How do I find out what the names of some of those works might be, if they do exist?

I also want to find out what musical instruments were invented just for avant-garde music. She played a few things that used the Moog synthesizer, but she also said that the synthesizer was being used for more mainstream music as well. Who invented the Moog synthesizer? Did they invent it specifically for avant-garde music, or for some other reason?

Although my instructor did not play any selections by this person, she did mention some woman from Europe who developed playing the inside of the piano. I'm interested in finding out a little more about this person, and what sorts of performance techniques she uses. I especially want to know what instruments or tools she uses to play the inside of a piano, and what she considers to be the "inside." Does that mean only strings, or does it also mean nuts and bolts and glue and boards?

And what about chance music? Is there a difference between chance music and avant-garde music? How did chance music get its start?

One thing I'm interested in too is what people's re-action to avant-garde music has been. Do most people like it? Do most musicians like it? What about music critics? What do they think about it?

Compared to other types of music, is avant-garde music more difficult to perform? Does the sheet music look all that different from regular sheet music? Where could I find some sheet music or scores or whatever they are called for avant-garde-type music?

Has anyone made any predictions for what the future of avant-garde music might be? Or the future of music in general?

FINE ARTS

FINE ARTS

Questions

Please provide a complete bibliographic citation for at least one source that will provide an answer to each of the following questions.

1. Is Claes Oldenburg still alive?

2. Has Salvador Dali really written a cookbook? What is the title, and how much does it cost?

3. What does the term "sepia" mean?

4. What is an aquatint?

5. Is it very difficult to do a batik?

6. What is the difference between batik and tie-dyeing?

7. Who is considered to be the best painter of the Italian Renaissance?

8. Is there any way that I could get a copy of Rembrandt's Nightwatch?

9. Does the Detroit Institute of Arts own any works by Leonardo de Vinci?

10. Who designed Notre Dame Cathedral?

11. What is Dadaism? Does it have any relationship with Surrealism?

12. Are there any good books written about the life of

Georgia O'Keeffe? I would like one that has color reproductions.

13. How many members of the Peale family were portraitists?

14. How many were miniaturists?

15. Are there any graduate schools that offer an M. F. A. degree in photography?

16. How much exhibit space is there at the Metropolitan Museum of Art?

17. Did Mark Rothko ever write about his philosophy of art?

18. Who is generally regarded to be the first art historian?

19. How many separate art libraries are there in the United States?

20. Who is Ansel Adams?

21. Has Louise Nettleson ever had a show in New York? Where could I locate reactions of critics to her work?

22. What is a flying buttress?

23. Is it true that Frank Lloyd Wright's mother hung pictures of architects and buildings in her home while she was pregnant with him?

24. When was the French Academy of Art begun? Who is the current president or director?

25. What is the largest amount of money ever paid for a sculpture?

26. What is the address of the Commission of Fine Arts?

27. Who invented the skyscraper?

28. What materials are necessary to do scrimshaw?

29. I need a book on how to open and operate an art gallery. Can you recommend one?

30. Why is the Virgin Mary usually painted in blue clothing?

31. Who was the greatest art forger of all time?

32. Are holograms art?

33. How long has the Freer Gallery been in existence? Does it have any special collections?

34. The East Wing of the National Gallery of Art houses a rather large mobile that was done by Alexander Calder before his death. Is there any way I could find out how much this work weighs; and how long it took Calder to make the mobile?

35. Who painted La Giaconda? Was the subject of the painting a real person?

36. If an artist donated a work of art to a museum, how much of a tax deduction would he or she be allowed to take?

37. What does the indication "51/250" mean when it appears on an engraving?

38. What is the function of cones in a firing kiln?

39. What is the chemical composition of clay?

40. Is collage really a recognized art form? When and where was it begun?

41. At the time of his death, how many works by Picasso were still in his possession?

42. How many of the presidents of the United States have been "Sunday painters"?

43. Who is considered to have written the most comprehensive biography of Toulouse-Lautrec? Was the work either written or translated into English?

44. Why did Velasquez include so many dwarfs or midgets in his paintings?

45. How many self-portraits did Vincent van Gogh paint?

46. Who were the major American primitive painters?

47. Which school of art is Andy Warhol generally credited with having started?

48. In December 1951, police in Pittsfield, Massachusetts, banned an issue of Time magazine from the newsstands, due to the reproduction of a work of art. What was the work? What about it was found to be objectionable?

49. Whatever became of the nude statue of Pocahontas that caused such a furor at the Louisiana State Museum in 1953.

50. In 1978, a drawing by Maurice de Vlaminck entitled Le pêcheur was sold at auction. What was the medium? What price did it bring?

51. On May 18, 1978, Sotheby Parke Bernet auctioned a bronze sculpture by Jasper Johns. The work brought $30,000. What was it's title?

52. Who painted Gathering in the Country near a Statue of a Seated Woman?

53. Raphael painted a work entitled Psyche Carried to Heaven by the Breezes. In what year was it painted?

54. In Northern Renaissance painting, does a dog symbolize anything?

55. Have any paintings been done of Zuni rain dancers?

56. In what area of the fine arts is Eugene Durieu known? Where could I find copies of what he has done?

57. Where could I find a copy of Harold Edgerton's photograph of Splash of Milk Resulting from the Dropping of a Ball, Which Is Seen on the Rebound?

58. Who invented the camera?

59. Who invented the camera obscura?

60. Who is the best contemporary Japanese art photographer?

61. Does Emile Zola have any reputation as a photographer?

62. Where could I find photographs of floods?

63. What kind of camera does Ansel Adams use?

64. Where could I locate geographical information about A. T. H. Boehm, a Finnish painter and graphic artist?

65. What is the difference in style between French Provincial and Queen Anne furniture?

66. Of what nationality was Sophie Nelson Brosnan, a painter of the 19th century?

67. Who developed lithography as an art form?

68. Are there any collections of photographs of royal crowns and other headgear?

69. In what medium has Georgiana Brown Harbeson worked?

70. Who were the best-known American cartoonists of the 18th century?

71. Why has the Madonna been such a popular subject of painters and sculptors?

72. Were there any female artists during the Italian Renaissance?

73. How many federal government agencies are specifically concerned with promoting the fine arts in the United States?

74. Have there been any exhibitions of American folk art during the past year?

75. Does the Louvre publish any serials that contain articles about its collections?

76. Where could I get some information about recent excavations of Art in Egypt?

77. K. A. Giles did a dissertation about the Strozzi Chapel in Santa Maria Novella. When was the dissertation done? Was it ever published in summary form as an article?

78.   Where could I get some information, along with illus-
        trations, on basket-making and blankets of the Indians
        of North America?

79.   Within the past few years Peter Knapp wrote an article
        about Peter Lindbergh. What was the subject of the
        article? Where did it appear?

80.   Where could I find out who the most famous 20th-
        century book designers are?

81.   How much has been written about Catalan Gothic archi-
        tecture?

82.   Is the Art Students League of New York still in ex-
        istence?

83.   I need to find an article or book that discusses in de-
        tail any difference between American pennies made
        from 1793 to 1814.

84.   Who is credited with having first designed Chippendale
        furniture?

85.   Are there any children's museums in Tennessee?

86.   Where could I find a brief history of the National Gal-
        lery?

87.   Is art a good investment against inflation?

88.   I want to find a recent article about German glass
        painting and staining.

89.   What significance did WPA have for the arts?

90.   How could I find some articles about Blacks in art
        during the 1940's?

91.   When was the Newark Museum founded? What are its
        special collections?

92.   Are there any museums of erotic art in the United
        States?

93.   Where is Sachem's Wood, one of the earliest Greek
        revival mansions in the United States?

94.   Why is Chinese art sometimes classed by dynasty?

95.   I would like to find some criticism about Nazi art, particularly sculpture.

96.   Where could I locate early city plans for Detroit?

97.   What do you call a person who designs coffins?

98.   In 1941, Jakob Rosenberg wrote an article about recent acquisitions of the department of prints for some museum.   Which museum was it?

99.   Where could I locate information about the aesthetics of bathroom design?

100. Have any libraries won awards for their architectural design?

101. What are the major divisions of classifications of Minoan Art?

102. Who were "Les Fauvistes"?

103. Where could I find a review of English Gardens and Landscapes, 1700-1750, by C. Hussey?

104. What was De Stijl?

105. How do I go about making a frame?

106. Has any of John Constable's correspondence been published?

107. I would like complete bibliographic information for a book by P. Colin titled La Peinture belge depuis 1830.

108. How many computerized data bases exist in the field of art?

109. Where could I locate abstracts of articles dealing with art education?

110. Who is the best living authority on Jain iconography?

111. What inspired Rouault's Veronica's Veil?

112. Why are all the books about Picasso not classed together in the Library of Congress classification scheme?

113. Who designed the Colosseum?

114. What is the most prestigious national award for art in the United States?

115. Were any members of the Medici family artists?

116. Why does Michelangelo's statue of Moses have horns?

117. Which museum owns Thomas Eakins' The Writing Master?

118. Which American artists exhibited at the Salon des Refusés?

119. What exactly are the minor arts?

120. I need a copy of the Commercial Standard for Artists' Oil Paints CS 98-62.

121. How thick is Bristol board?

122. Who invented the color wheel?

123. Who was Picasso's favorite model?

124. When did psychedelic art first become popular in the U.S. ?

125. Are there any manuals of calligraphy written for left-handed people?

126. Where could I find a how-to-do-ceramics book for children?

127. What were the seven wonders of the ancient world?

128. Are there any Spanish-English, English-Spanish art dictionaries?

129. How many art galleries are there in Guatemala?

130. Who is Sotheby Parke Bernet's representative in Australia?

131. Where could I find a list of paintings that are at the White House?

132. Where are the major collections of Futurism in the United States?

133. Are Andrew Wyeth and Jamie Wyeth related?

134. What is the best reproduction of the Book of Kells?

135. Do the floor plans of most churches resemble a cross?

136. Who is the leading figure in commercial art?

137. How much does a good fashion photographer earn in a year?

138. How did the image of the artist as a starving Bohemian get started?

139. Where could I find a review of Signs and Symbols in Christian Art, by Ferguson?

140. What is the largest association of professional painters in the United States?

141. From whom could I order some slides of works by Manet?

142. What is distinctive about the technique of pointillism?

143. I need to locate some examples of "trompe l'oeil."

144. How many volumes are there in the Pelican History of Art series?

145. Are there any reproductions of works of art available in microform?

146. Who is the curator of the Freer Gallery?

147. Does the Chicago Art Institute have any collections of the French Impressionists?

148. What is calendar art?

149. For how many years did Paul Gauguin live in Tahiti?

150. What is the real title of Whistler's Mother?

FINE ARTS

Search Problems

A. As the serials librarian in a medium-sized public library, you are asked by the director to evaluate current titles the library is receiving. She would also like you to suggest new titles that might be added in a few areas not currently covered. One of these areas is fine arts. The memo you receive requests that you supply, with annotations, a list of ten periodical titles that would be best to aid the information and recreational needs of a diverse community which at present has no museums or galleries or collections of fine arts. In addition to the annotations, you must also rate the periodicals from 1 to 10, indicating the priority in which they should be received. How would you proceed in supplying the information? Which ten titles would you list?

B. I saw a report on the television a while back about art forgers and forgeries, and how it really is a pretty big business for the people involved. I want to find out a little more information about the subject, if you have any here. Does anyone know where the center of art forgery is? I mean, is it here in the United States, or do most forgeries come from Europe or someplace else? What was the highest price paid for a work of art that was later discovered to be a forgery? Are most of the forgers established artists who sell their own art through normal channels, or do they spend all of their time doing forgeries? I know painting is the big area of forgery, but are there forgeries of other media as well, like sculpture or pottery or drawings?

C. My husband and I are going to be making a trip through Canada next spring, visiting the major cities--Quebec, Montreal, Ottawa, Toronto, and Vancouver. We have long been fans of folksy-type art, and would like to find some Canadian folk art while we are there. The only problem is that we don't know where to look. Are there special galleries in any of these cities that have large collections of Canadian folk art? We also want to find and buy some Eskimo art if we can. Is that considered to be folk art in Canada, or is that ethnic art? How would we go about finding where we could get some Eskimo art? Also, we don't want to pay too much for something. How can I find out what the going price of some items might be?

D. My great-aunt died a few months back, and left her three nephews part of her collection of 19th-century French prints and drawings. None of us ever really liked the collection anyway, but now I own four things that I would just as soon get rid of. I can't hang them, because they would clash horribly with the hard-edge paintings I have. What I would really like to know is how much they might be worth, so that I can either sell them, or give them away and take their value as a tax write-off. One of the works is a cartoon drawing signed by somebody named Daumier, who I never heard of. Two others look a little bit like posters, or sketches for posters. They are signed by somebody named Lautrec. The fourth one is an etching by somebody named either Monet or Manet. The print is too small for me to read. How much do you think they might be worth?

E. I'm interested in finding out how much more attention and recognition is being given to female artists in this country during the past decade as compared with the decade before that. I thought one way of finding out what I want to know is to find out how many separate exhibitions there have been of women painters during both periods of time. Are there any books or lists somewhere of exhibition catalogs which would list those exhibitions? Or should I try to find out some other way? Do you think anybody has done any studies about this? Or written any articles that could help me?

F. I want to get some information on antiques, if you have it. Not all antiques, just furniture. Especially dining room chairs and buffets. Basically, what I need is a book that will have photographs of different chairs and buffets from different time periods, and that talks about different styles and stuff like that. I have some odds and ends packed away in the attic to my garage, which I put there when we got a new dining room suite about twenty-five years ago. Since it was all furniture that my mother's father's family used, I figure it must be about one hundred years old. Oh, one other thing. Are there any books that explain how you can tell where a piece of furniture was made? Like in what country?

G.   I have been reading a lot about Russian history lately,
especially biography.   And one interesting thing that I keep
coming across is the custom, which apparently reached it's
peak with Nicholas and Alexandra, of exchanging beautiful
Easter eggs.   Well, the books I have read describe some of
these eggs in great detail, but they never have any photographs
so that you can see what they looked like.   How could I find
some photographs, preferably in color?   You know, some of
them were done by some man named Fabergé, who I think
was a jeweler.   Maybe some of them might be in a book
about him.   Apparently, some of the eggs are still around
somewhere.   Is there any way I could find out where they
are, or if they are in any museums?

H.   You know, every time you go to a museum, you see a
lot of really nice paintings and sculpture, especially the older
stuff.   And then you come across a lot of this modern jazzy
art that looks like somebody threw a plate of green and blue
and red spaghetti on a canvas, and then sat on it.   I just
don't understand it, none of it.   Well, I made the same kind
of remark when I was at the museum last week with a few
friends; and one of them said that maybe I should go to the
library and find some sort of book that could explain it all
to me.   So here I am.   Do you have any books that will do
that?   I mean, I really want to know what makes a person
paint stuff like that.   Are they trying to say something?   If
they are, what are they trying to say?

I.   I want to find some information on teaching art appreciation, particularly to the elderly.   Our local volunteer group
is trying to set up a program so that we can go around to
different nursing homes and convalescent centers here in the
city, and give little slide shows and talks about art and artists.   We think that the people really want to have something
like this; but at the same time we do not want to bore them,
or do it on a level which is too elementary or too advanced.
What would be the best way to get the information?   Is there
any way of finding out if other programs like this have been
done around the country?   And how successful they were?

J.   In celebration of Gertrude Stein's birthday, Gwendolyn
Holbrook has decided to present a brief slide/tape demonstration and discussion of the relationship between Gertrude Stein
and Pablo Picasso.   Unfortunately, her exposure to the works
of both individuals has been somewhat limited.   For the purposes of the presentation, she would like to present concise
biographical material on each individual, focusing upon the

relationship, both biographical and creative, that each individual shared with the other. Ms. Holbrook is particularly
concerned in reciting those works of Gertrude Stein that show
the influence of Picasso, and displaying those works of Picasso that show the influence of Stein. Since both names
have been identified with Cubism, it will also be necessary
to give a brief history of this movement in painting as well
as in literature. How would you proceed in satisfying Ms.
Holbrook's needs relative to this subject?

K. An undergraduate student arrives at the reference desk
seeking information for a project in her art history course.
She remembers reading about the Armory Show that was held
in New York and wants to know more about it. Specifically,
she needs to know the year that it was held, whether the works
of any American artists were shown, and what the general reaction of the public was at the time of the show. She would
also like to make a list of some of the artists whose work
was exhibited and the titles of some of the works exhibited.
Finally, she needs to know if reproductions of any of these
works are available.

L. I was just looking at some book about women artists and
it mentioned a few groups and publications that I would like
to know a little about. All it gave in the book was the names,
no other information. The groups or places that were mentioned are: Women's Interart Center, Inc.; Ad Hoc Women
Artists; AIA Task Force on Women; Women's International
Network; and Women's Art Center. Where could I find out
more about these groups, like where they are located, when
they first started, and exactly what they do or why they exist?
Two publications that were mentioned are Feminist Art Journal of Liberation and Women Artists' Newsletter. Again, I
would like their address and when they started publishing, and
some information about what kind of material is published in
these two publications.

M. A friend of mine was telling me a little bit about these
two Black artists that she said I might enjoy ... that I might
like some of the subject matter of their works. Their names
are Archibald J. Motley, Jr., and Robert Reid. I assume
that they are still living, but I'm not really sure. What I
want to know about them is what kind of art did they do.
Were they painters or sculptors or what? I would also like
to find out some basic biographical information about them,
including the names of some of the things they have done and
where and when there might have been any exhibitions of their

works. Are there any special collections of their works anywhere in this country? What about awards? Have either of
them won any awards? Finally, are they important enough
so that somebody may have written up something about them
or their works, even if it is only an article?

N. Whenever I go in an art store I notice that they have all
these different kinds of paper made for artists, but there
aren't any signs around that explain what any of it is, or
what it should be used for. I asked the clerk, but she didn't
seem to know but a few kinds. Do you have anything here
at the library that explains the different kinds of paper that
are produced for artists, and which paper should be used for
which kind of art? I want to· make up some note cards, some
with just plain pen and ink, and some others with linoleum
blocks and inks. But I don't want to buy the wrong paper for
what I have to do.

O. Do you have any books here that have something to do
with Japanese art? I was in a gallery a few weeks ago, and
there was an exhibition of some 19th-century Japanese prints.
I was really fascinated by the subject matter and the technique
or whatever. What struck me most was that there really is
a big difference between how Japanese art looks and how American art looks. What I want to know is why. Do the Japanese
have such different styles of drawing and painting and printmaking, or was the show that I saw just a fluke? What I
would like to find is either a history of Japanese art or maybe
something that explains the basic principles or philosophies
of Japanese artists.

P. A friend of mine who is an artist is beginning to do some
work with art and with mental patients. She says that the
field of art therapy is pretty new, at least in terms of what
she is doing. I'm kind of interested in finding out a little
bit more about this. Who is qualified to do something like
art therapy? Is it an artist or a psychiatrist? Is there a
lot of art therapy being done in this country? Is it a relatively new field, or has art therapy been used in other places
at other times? How does the art world react to something
like this?

Q. I'm toying with the idea of maybe going into some sort
of business, and I thought that it might be a lot of fun to try
my hand at running an art gallery. Unfortunately, I really
have not had any experience with that sort of thing; and I
figure that before I start making any plans I had better see

how much work and how much profit would be involved in
something like that. Are there any books or something,
maybe a manual, that explains very clearly how to open and
manage an art gallery? Basically, I would like to know how
much space you need, or should have, to have an adequate
gallery. I also need to know how to go about finding artists
who are willing to show their works in a gallery. Do most
galleries specialize in one type of art, or do they pretty much
have general collections? Are there any statistics on how
much money can be made by running a gallery?

R. We have to do a paper for this art history course that
I'm taking, and my instructor said that it would be all right
with him if I did mine on the general field of art criticism.
What I want to do is trace the history of art criticism from
whenever it began up to the present day. It doesn't have to
be a long, footnoted paper, but I do want to trace any major
schools of art criticism. I couldn't find a whole lot of information in the textbook we are using for the class. Where
could I find out who started art criticism? Are there different schools of art criticism, or is it all pretty much the
same? If there are different schools or ideas, is there any
place that would list these all, or do I have to go to a bunch
of different places?

S. One thing I'm curious about is how an artist determines
how much a certain piece of art is worth. I know to some
extent that that is based upon the reputation of an artist, but
still there must be some sort of guidelines, aren't there?
Or does an artist just price something at a price that he or
she thinks people are willing to pay? And why are some
works by artists worth so much more than other works by
the same artist? Does the reaction of critics have anything
to do with that? And why does the price of any artist's work
go up so much when they die?

T. I keep coming across this term "iconography" in the art
history books that I have been looking at, and I'm starting to
get confused by it. I thought that icons were those kinds of
portraits of saints and other holy people that were found in
Russian churches. But I guess I'm wrong. What does that
term mean? Are there different meanings associated with it?
And how can you tell when someone is using the word in a
certain way, or to mean a certain thing? Are the terms
"icon" and "iconography" related? Does either term apply to
any fields other than art?

U. Our local library recently put on exhibit a few examples of manuscripts and manuscript illumination which someone had donated to the Rare Book Room. I was just amazed. Those pictures that go along with the manuscripts are just so beautiful! And they are in such good shape for being so old. How could I find out how people did those little paintings, especially the kind that are inside of a letter of the alphabet? How long did it take them to paint those? And the colors that they used--they are just all so beautiful. Is there any way I can find out what they did to make those colors? Would I be able to mix up the same colors at home?

FINE ARTS

Case Studies

I. I have to do a lengthy paper for a 20th-century art course
that I am taking, and the person that I really want to write
about is Picasso. I have read a few biographies of him, and
lots of magazine articles. He obviously was one of the most
important and influential artists of the 20th century; and because of that, there is just so much material about him and
his art that I don't know where to begin.

I have kind of jotted down some notes on different areas that
I want to find out about. Once I get all the information together, I figure that I'll be in a better position to know exactly what it is that I want to write.

First of all, what I need to get notes on is just pure and
simple biographical information, including his birth and death
dates, where he grew up, where he went to school, what sort
of formal art training he had, how old he was when he first
started to create, who he married, what the names of his
children were, and all the places he has lived and worked.

I also want to find a complete list of all the awards that he
won while he was alive.

        I know that Picasso painted and sculpted and did some
printmaking and drawing. What I need to know is all of the
media in which the artist created. Did he do any mobiles or
multi-media works?

        I remember hearing at one time that not everything
that was signed with Picasso's name was actually done by
him. Does that mean that they were forgeries?

        You know, a lot of things I read about Picasso kind
of divide up his life into different periods, according to the

type of things he did. Like a Blue period and a Red period. Where could I find a list or something that would tell me what all the different periods or styles were?

Has anyone ever estimated, or is there an exact total of all the works that the artist produced?

Just for my own interest, I would like to know how much money he made during his lifetime.

When exactly did the name Picasso hit the art scene? What I mean is, how long had he been painting before he actually got some sort of recognition from the art world? And was there one specific work that started the ball rolling?

Did he ever indicate which were his favorite works? Either the ones that he liked the best, or the ones that he enjoyed doing the most?

Since he lived such a long time, and created so many different things, he must have gone through a lot of models. Have any of the models who posed for Picasso written any impressions of what it was like to work for the artist?

What other famous names in art did Picasso count among his closest friends?

What exactly was it that the art critics liked so much about Picasso? Was it his sense of design? Or the subject matter of his works? Or the style of the artist?

Rather than read a whole lot of books and articles about him, it would probably save me some time if I could find abstracts of things that have been written. How easy are those to come by? And where would I look to see if they even existed?

I know there is a famous sculpture by Picasso some-where in Chicago. Where could I find out what other sculp-tures done by him are in the United States--not in private collections, but in public places?

Where could I find out what the best biographies of Picasso are--you know, those that deal with all aspects of his life?

II. I'm exploring possible topics for a thesis in anthropology, and the area I am most interested in right now is the American Indian. I know that that is a pretty broad topic, and that I will probably have to narrow it down somewhat to a few specific tribes, or groups of tribes. What I want to explore is the area of American Indian art; but before I get too deep into the area, I would like to find out what has already been done. I may have to end up not only limiting the thesis to specific tribes, but also specific types of art or crafts.

First of all, I am going to need to find a list of all theses and dissertations which have been done in this area, whether they were accepted by anthropology departments or by art departments. Where could I go for that information? I will probably also need to find out, if it is at all possible, what topics have been accepted but have not yet been completed. I sure would hate to start up something and then not be able to do it because someone else beat me to it.

In addition to theses and dissertations, I will also need to know what books in general have been written pertaining to American Indian art. I am not really interested in those books that are just collections of photographs or prints of different kinds of art. What I need to know about right now are books which are either historical or analytical from an aesthetic or anthropological point of view. Do you know what I mean?

Eventually, I will need to look at collections of photographs and prints, but they probably will not be an adequate substitute for actually going to some museums and examining the works in person. Where could I find some sort of listing of museums or other special collections of American Indian art?

You know, I have heard about this one place called the Amerind Foundation which is somewhere in Arizona. A friend of mine mentioned that they might have a lot of the material that would be useful to me. Where could I find out more about that place? I'll need to know where it is located and exactly what it is all about. Are there other foundations or organizations which are similar to this one?

I suppose that as part of this, I am going to have to check lots and lots of bibliographies, too, just to make sure that I don't miss anything. But I'm not sure where to begin there, either. Would I do better to check a general bibliography of art and look under something like "American Indian," or would it be quicker to look for bibliographies which are concerned only with Indian art? I suppose that maybe I should check a few anthropology bibliographies too, just to see what they list on the subject; or do you think that they wouldn't have much?

I will also need to locate some information, or what has been written as far as criticism of Indian art. Since it seems to me that most American Indian art is folk art, there probably won't be too much written in terms of formal criticism. But if there is, where could I go to find out?

III. Our local Italian-American Club has collected an awful lot of donations over the years which we had set aside for some special occasion when we might need it. As you know, the past president has recently died; and at the last member-ship meeting it was decided that we should use some of that money to do something of a memorial nature for him. One of the members has suggested that we have a statue built. Another member said that maybe we should give it to the library for memorial books.

After a long debate over the matter, we decided that we would either purchase a work of art, or have one made, in honor of this man. Now, of course, we have the problem of deciding which work of art we want. We have $5,000 to spend; and the only other restriction is that the artist be an Italian-American, and that the subject matter be of interest to the Italian-American community.

I have been elected Chairman of the committee that will be handling this, so I came down here to the library to see what sort of information I could find. There are a few local art-ists that are members of our club; but so that there would not be any friction or fighting over the project, we decided that we would not ask any of them to do anything for us ex-cept for maybe giving their opinions on the final choice.

So what I need from the library, if you have it here, are the names of some Italian-American artists who are either still living or who made some sort of name for them-selves while they were still alive. Where could I get that information? Would it take long?

Right now, we are not very particular whether the

final work is a painting or a sculpture, or whatever, just as long as it is nice and we can buy it for under $5,000. But I really don't even know what direction to go in. Once I find the names of these different people, how am I going to find out what kinds of things they did?

Do most listings of artists also give their home addresses, or some other way that we could get in touch with them if we wanted to?

How are we going to find pictures or something of the various works that these artists have done? If they are so famous that we could find them in any textbook, then we probably are not going to be able to afford them.

Maybe we could try going through some galleries or museums. Is that generally a good idea, or do you end up paying more than if you just bought the work directly from the artist?

Are there any galleries or museums that might have special collections of Italian-American artists?

What about art schools? Maybe we could write off to some of them to find some up-and-coming students of Italian background. But I don't know of any art schools here in Tennessee. Can you give me the names of some of the bigger ones?

How do we know how much we should pay an artist for a particular work? If we see something in a gallery that we like, and it has a price, that shouldn't be any problem. But if we decide to have something made, do most artists haggle over prices, or do they just say how much they will charge, and that's that? And will we have the right to refuse it if we don't like the finished product?

IV. I want to locate some information on some of the museums in New York City. My family is planning a vacation there in about three months, and I know that I will not be very interested in doing most of the things that they want to do. So I figured I would kind of set up my own little agenda of places to visit and things to see.

The two museums that I want to be sure to visit are the Metropolitan Museum of Art and the Museum of Modern

Art. Basically what I need to know about them is when they are open, and how close they are to each other.

Are they very big museums? What I want to know is how much time I should plan on spending at either one of them. Is there any way I could find out how many different things they have on exhibit, as well as how much floor space there is to cover?

I would also like to know what the special collections of either museum are. Are they both pretty much the same, in terms of collections?

Has anything been written about the history of either museum? Like how old it is, and how many pieces or items they had when they first began? And how the collection has developed over the years? I think that might be interesting.

I mentioned my trip to my friends, and they said to be sure to stop by the Cloisters and the Frick and the Guggenheim and the Whitney as well. Well, I have never heard of these other places, but if they are interesting places, I sure don't want to miss them. What could I find out here about those places? Are they museums? If they are, then I would like to know what their hours are, too. And, if you can tell me, I'd like to know what special collections they have that might make a visit to them worthwhile.

Does New York have the most museums of any city in the United States?

Are there any other important museums that are in New York that I should know about for my trip?

THEATER ARTS

THEATER ARTS

Please provide a complete bibliographic citation for at least one source that will provide an answer to each of the following questions.

Theater and Costume

1. Before Helen Hayes, who was considered to be the First Lady of the American Theater?

2. When and where was the proscenium arch developed?

3. Did Aristophanes write anything other than comedies?

4. Where do actors learn dialects?

5. What is Actors Equity?

6. Where could I locate illustrations of Latvian peasant dress during the 17th century?

7. Where could I find a history of wigs and wigmaking?

8. What were the names of the original cast of Waiting for Godot?

9. Who is the most influential theater critic in the United States?

10. Who owns the Ringling Brothers Circus?

11. Are there any archives of the early days of burlesque?

12. What was the function of the chorus in ancient Greek drama?

13. How many plays have been written about Oedipus?

14. Where could I find illustrations of chastity belts?

15. When and where did the tie come into vogue as a part of male apparel?

16. What is the difference between commedia dell'arte and commedia erudita?

17. Who was the best-known designer of hats in France during the 19th-century?

18. When were the Toni Awards started?

19. Where could I find some articles about different techniques of stage lighting?

20. Is stage left at the audience's left or the actor's left?

21. What is the oldest theater auditorium in the country?

22. What is the earliest known play to have been performed in English?

23. What is the difference between Broadway, off-Broadway, and off-off-Broadway?

24. Where is the Guthrie Theater?

25. Who was the first woman to play Camille on the stage?

26. I'd like a diagram of early Roman theaters.

27. Do any of Shakespeare's plays incorporate a masque?

28. What is "deus ex machina"?

29. Have any books been written about the Federal Theatre Project?

30. When did the Community Theater movement begin in the United States?

31. When and where was the study of theater first intro-

duced into the curriculum of the American college or university?

32. Does Wayne State University have a resident theater?

33. When was the first production of Showboat?

34. Who wrote The Reverend Griffith Davenport?

35. What have the critics' reactions been to Ceremonies in Dark Old Men?

36. Are there any feminist theater cooperatives in the United States?

37. Has Glenda Jackson ever appeared in a play on Broadway?

38. Have galoshes ever been fashionable?

39. For which theater in Toronto did Marc Chagall design a stage curtain?

40. What are the functions of a producer?

41. How long has Variety been in existence?

42. Are there any books about costuming that include designs and directions for how to make the costumes?

43. Did Raisin in the Sun have any significance in the history of American theater?

44. Are there any theater schools that specialize in training child actors?

45. Where could I find illustrations of performances of Our American Cousin?

46. What is a flat-fell seam?

47. Is it very hard to make a feather boa? How much would it cost?

48. What is the name of the community theater in Columbia, South Carolina?

49. Where could I find a discussion with illustrations of various beard styles for men?

50. Did Marie Antoinette really have wigs that had model boats in them?

51. Where could I get some information about classical puppet theater in Japan?

52. Why do plays have intermissions?

53. What was so distinctive about Stanislavsky's method of acting?

54. Has much been written about the philosophy of fashion?

55. What is the difference between a puppet and a marionette?

56. What are the advantages and disadvantages of theater in the round?

57. Where could I locate reviews of the latest edition of Phyllis Hartnoll's Oxford Companion to the Theatre?

58. Where can I find a list of all dissertations done in Canada about Canadian theater?

59. I need to find a glossary of costume terms.

60. How large is the Research Library of the Performing Arts of New York Public Library?

61. Are there any museums of costume in the United States?

62. What is the current address of the International Guild of Prestidigitators?

63. Where could I get some information about staging plays for children?

64. What are the major serial publications of the International Theatre Institute?

65. Are there any organizations dedicated to the study of circus history?

66. Where could I go to school to learn to be a clown?

67. Is there any sort of theater library association in the United States or England?

68. Where could I find a good history of Mexican theater?

69. Where could I locate reviews of The Man Who Came to Dinner?

70. When was the "Golden Age" of the Broadway musical?

71. Is World Theatre a bilingual publication?

72. How many computerized data bases exist for the performing arts?

73. Are there any theater magazines designed for children?

74. How many different recordings of Hamlet are available?

75. What was La Salle des Machines?

76. Who was Le Petomane?

77. Who are the most significant Russian playwrights alive today?

78. What has been the influence of German theater upon American theater?

79. Where could I find a list of plays about the Vietnam Conflict?

80. Was the corset invented by a man or by a woman?

81. Where could I find pictures of different academic caps and gowns?

82. What is the average price for a ticket to a popular Broadway play?

83. What does the French term "échec" mean?

84. When did women first start coloring their hair?

85. What is the origin of the expression "That's show business"?

86. Where could I find some plays with three female roles?

87. Where could I learn how to write plays?

88. How important are masks in Kabuki drama?

89. Does Grove Press publish any plays?

90. Who holds production rights to Oklahoma?

91. Have any religious plays been written for child performers?

92. What awards has Annie won?

93. What was the longest-running play on Broadway?

94. What was the longest-running play off Broadway?

95. Has Mae West written any plays? Have they ever been performed?

96. Where could I find some pictures of balloon dresses and pill-box hats?

97. Where could I get information about Tibetan religious theater?

98. Where is the Barter Theater? Does it have any significance?

99. How long has Paris been considered the center of high fashion?

100. Have there been any famous plays written about costume or fashion designers?

Dance, Film, Television

1. Who wrote the screenplay for Gone with the Wind?

2. What is a pas de deux?

3. Was Hollywood always the center of the American motion-picture industry?

4. What contributions did Isadora Duncan make to the field of dance?

5. What is the exact running time of From Here to Eternity?

6. Where could I find a list of full-length feature films about vampires?

7. How many films has Henry Fonda made?

8. What were the most popular television programs in 1957?

9. Who can vote for the Academy Awards?

10. Where could I locate criticism of Truffaut as a director?

11. Who is the best male dancer alive today?

12. What is Benesh notation?

13. What formal training is expected of a choreographer?

14. Has Merce Cunningham written anything about his philosophy of dancing?

15. Who played the role of Ethel Mertz in the "I Love Lucy" television program?

16. What is the membership size of the National Association for Regional Ballet?

17. How many Academy Awards have been won by the Walt Disney studios?

18. What was the first full-length feature sound motion picture?

19. Has Nureyev ever danced with the Royal Winnipeg Ballet?

20. Who played the lead roles in the film The Turning Point?

21. How long has the New York City Ballet been in existence?

22. What were the contributions of Jean Dauberval to the field of dance?

23. Who is the director for the recent film version of <u>Don Giovanni</u>?

24. What is the best biography of Vaslav Nijinsky?

25. Are Russian dancers superior to dancers of other nations?

26. When and where was "la volta" in vogue?

27. Where could I find out how to do "the bump"?

28. Has René Clair written any reflections on his years in film?

29. Was Marilyn Monroe working on a film when she died?

30. Does the American Film Institute have any stated goals and objectives?

31. Who holds the rights to Charlie Chaplin's films?

32. Where could I find information on Italian folk dances of the 17th century?

33. I would like to find some articles written within the past few years on the subject of religion and dance.

34. What is labanotation?

35. What are the seven principal movements in classical ballet?

36. How do dancers communicate?

37. Who are the film directors associated with the New Wave?

38. What does "framing" mean as it applies to filming?

39. How tall is Paul Newman?

40. How many films did the Barrymores make in which they all appeared?

41.   What is the most popular television Western of all time?

42.   Did Paddy Chayefsky ever write anything for "The Twilight Zone"?

43.   What term is used to refer to a dancer's ability to stay in the air during a leap?

44.   Can you recommend a good book to teach dance to children?

45.   How many members are there in the Federation of Motion Picture Councils?

46.   Who publishes Film Critic?

47.   Does Penguin Books publish any series devoted to films?

48.   Who determines what credits will be listed at the beginning of a film?

49.   What is the largest film society in France?

50.   Who is the leading female star of films in India?

51.   Do most cinematographers have to be licensed?

52.   I would like to find some recent articles about Bharata Natya.

53.   Where could I locate up-to-date biographical information on Juliet Prowse?

54.   Who was the star of She Done Him Wrong?

55.   Where could I locate critical reaction to Pink Flamingos?

56.   What is the longest film that Andy Warhol made?

57.   How many books by John Steinbeck have been made into movies?

58.   Who was the first movie cowboy to have a large following?

59. To what does the term "special effects" refer?

60. Was Oedipus the King ever made into a movie?

61. Where could I find out what was the major national news story covered on CBS Evening News on March 15, 1978?

62. What is the status of the motion picture industry in Greenland?

63. I would like to find a lengthy discussion of homosexuality in films.

64. What could you recommend as a good dictionary of dance terms?

65. When critics evaluate a film, what areas are they most likely to talk about?

66. Are there any Spanish-language dance periodicals?

67. What is the difference between modern dance and classical dance?

68. For how long did Betty Ford study under Martha Graham?

69. What were the production costs for Cleopatra, starring Elizabeth Taylor?

70. Does Cinema Studies contain book reviews and film reviews?

71. Are there any good French dictionaries of ballet?

72. How many different types of square dancing are there?

73. Who produces the "Dance in America" television series?

74. Where could I find a history of ballroom dancing?

75. What was the Black Bottom?

76. Does Hammer Films specialize in any particular type of film?

77. Which actor and actress have won the most Academy Awards?

78. If Vivien Leigh had not played Scarlett O'Hara in Gone with the Wind, who would have played that role?

79. Why is Grauman's Chinese Theatre so significant to the movie industry?

80. Why are the Nielsen ratings important?

81. How many times has Liz Taylor been married?

82. Where could I write to Marlon Brando?

83. How many individual drawings are usually made for a five-minute animated film?

84. Who decides which films a studio will make?

85. Who invented the motion picture?

86. Are there any automated data bases of film literature?

87. Why is the Cannes Film Festival so important?

88. Was Network a pretty accurate portrayal of the television industry?

89. Who were the founders of United Artists?

90. Where could I locate a summary of The Nutcracker?

91. What are the circulation figures for American Cinematographer?

92. Were Fred Astaire and Ginger Rogers both trained to be dancers?

93. Who wrote the music for The Thomas Crown Affair?

94. How frequently is Hollywood Reporter published?

95. What were the circumstances of Ramon Navarro's death?

96. How many films has Bergman directed?

97. Do Fellini and Antonioni basically have the same philosophy of films and film-making?

98. Who played the female lead in the film production of Cabaret?

99. What were the ten best films of 1975?

100. What is the most prestigious dance award in America?

THEATER ARTS

Search Problems

A. I am doing a term paper on "The American Theater
1940-1950. " As part of this paper, I would like to put this
decade of the American theater in perspective with the decades
which preceded it as well as those which came after. Where
could I find a basic introduction to the history of the American
theater? I am also interested in documenting which were the
most popular plays of this period. Where could I locate this
information? I must also discover who were the major the-
atrical stars during the 1940's, and which of them are still
alive today. Also, where could I locate illustrations of the-
atrical productions of this time period?

B. Our local Women's Garden Club is going to view the
Alvin Ailey Dance Company in early October and we would
like to gather some information on this particular dance company. In addition, we would like to know what we should be
looking for during this performance. How long has the Alvin
Ailey Company been in existence? What was their first crit-
ically acclaimed performance? How large is their dance company? Who is their choreographer? Where has the company
appeared during the last year? Where could I locate illustrations of their performances? What exactly is modern dance?
What are the elements of modern dance that one should be
noting during a modern dance performance? How does modern dance differ from classical dance? Where could I locate
reviews of the Alvin Ailey Dance Company performances?

C. Our local civic club would like to sponsor a film festival
featuring ten of the best film comedies that have come out of
Hollywood since the beginning of sound motion pictures. The
problem is that we just don't know where to begin. Where
could I locate a list of all of the comedies produced from
Hollywood since 1930? If I cannot locate such a list, how
should I proceed to find out which were the best comedies?

Must we order these films directly from Hollywood or can
we operate through a local distributor? Where could I locate
criticisms of these motion pictures? I would also like to discover who were the major Hollywood comedians during the
past fifty years. Did any of them ever win an Academy
Award for their performance in a film? Where could I locate a film biography of these individuals?

D. As the serials librarian in a medium-sized public library,
you are asked by the director to evaluate current titles the
library is receiving. She would also like you to suggest new
titles that might be added in a few areas not currently covered. Two of these areas are dance and film. The memo
requests that you supply, with annotations, a list of ten periodical titles that would be best to meet the information and recreational needs of a diverse community of approximately
100,000 people. In addition to the annotations, you must
also rate the periodicals from 1 to 10, indicating the priority in which they should be acquired. How would you proceed in supplying the information? Which ten titles would
you list?

E. For a theater course which I am taking, the instructor
wants us to do a brief paper and oral presentation pertaining
to one 20th-century American scene designer. My instructor
gave me four names from which I can choose: Robert E.
Jones, Ming Cho Lee, Howard Bay and Robin Wagner. Right
now, I don't know anything about them except their names.
Where could I go to find some basic biographical information,
including where they have studied and what important things
they have done? Is there any book here that might list all
the plays for which they have done scene design? We also
have to include some illustrations as part of our oral report,
so I'll need to find some of those, too. Where would I go
to find some criticism of what they all have done?

F. I'm interested in becoming a fashion designer, and maybe
designing for both men and women. Right now, I'm trying to
figure out where I should go to school to get a good sound
education in the field. Are there any directories of fashion
schools in the United States? Would they also be able to tell
me how much it would cost for the complete program? Maybe
I should try to find out where some noted designers went to
school. Is that easy to find? People like Calvin Klein, Yves
St. Laurent, and Gucci. I also want to find out whether it
would be better for me to go to a regular college and major
in art, or whether I should go to a school specifically geared
to training fashion designers.

G. I'd like to find some information on film festivals around
the world, particularly those which are international in scope.
I have heard of the Cannes Film Festival, but I guess I don't
understand why it is so important. Does a film really have
bigger box office figures if it wins an award at the Cannes
Film Festival? Well, what are the other major film festivals? Are there any that are more important than the Cannes
Film Festival? Where and when are these other festivals
held? Are there any that take place in either the Soviet Union
or China?

H. Me and a few of my friends are planning a Halloween
party and we decided that we want people to come dressed
in any costume from the period between World War I and
World War II. Well, the problem with that is that not everybody we have invited knows what people used to dress like
then. So I'm here to find some books and magazines that
might have lots and lots of pictures of how people looked at
that time. Do you have any books here that would be really
good to use? And what about magazine titles? Which magazines would be the best ones, or at least have the most pictures of fashions from that period?

I. I have heard a lot about experimental theater in the United
States and Canada, but I'm not real sure what that term means.
Where could I find a good definition which might help clear
things up for me? Is there really a whole lot being done
currently in experimental theater? Both in the United States
and Canada? Who are the playwrights that are writing for
experimental theater? Are there any French-Canadians among
them? Would it be possible to find some illustrations of some
of these experimental productions?

J. I know that Wallace Berry and Majorie Main played in a
number of films together; and Hollywood used to pair off male
and female stars over and over once they realized that together they were big box office attractions. Other than that
couple, and teams like Spencer Tracy and Katherine Hepburn,
where could I find out what other famous stars were paired
together over and over? Were most of the movies that these
couples made together serial-type movies? What I mean is,
did each movie just seem to be a continuation of the previous
movie, or did they all have different subjects in which the
actors played different kinds of characters?

K. I want to find some information on the influence of African folk dances on current Black American popular dance. I
doubt that there are any books about the subject, but if you

could find one for me I sure would appreciate it. I don't
even really know how I could go about finding out about this.
Do you think that maybe there might be one or two articles
written about the subject somewhere? How am I going to be
able to find those? If you could, I would also like to find
some articles or whatever that might include some illustrations as well as some explanations of dance steps.

L. I need to locate some pictures of different outfits that
have been worn by the military in the United States since the
time of the colonies to the present day. Basically, what I
want to do is compare how things have changed during the
time involved. Where could I find photos or drawings of what
men in the Navy, Army, Marines, and Air Force have worn
since Colonial times? I would also like to find some explanations regarding how you can tell different ranks in the military on the basis of the clothes that the people wear. Who
decides when it is time to make a change in uniforms? I
think it might also be interesting to find out what women's
uniforms looked like. Would I be able to find that out in the
same place as the other stuff?

M. Where could I find out what the major names are in the
field of choreography for Broadway musical productions? Is
it pretty much the same people who keep choreographing the
hit shows or are there a lot of people doing it? I would also
be interested in knowing what someone in that position might
be paid for the work involved. Would it also be possible to
find out what kinds of awards some of these people have won?

N. For a women's studies course which I am taking, I want
to do a paper comparing the different ways in which women have
dressed women as opposed to how men have dressed women.
Where should I begin? Do you think that somebody may have
written something about this already? What should I look
under in the card catalog? Maybe I could just choose the
names of five women and five men who have designed exclusively for women. But I don't think that I could come up
with a list of ten names. Where could I go to find some
names? Is it very difficult to find illustrations of some of
these designers' clothes?

O. I remember as a kid that I used to watch a lot of cowboys and cowboy shows on television; and it just seems to me
that the way cowboys used to look back then is not the way
they look now on television. People like Hopalong Cassidy,
Gene Autry, Roy Rogers just don't seem like some of the

characters that are on the screen today. Am I right? Has
the image of the cowboy on television changed very much?
And what about Blacks? You know, you never see too many
Blacks as cowboys. Weren't there any Black cowboys back
in the Old West?

P. Where could I find some information on developments in
the American theater which happened as a result of general
cultural technological advancements? My instructor keeps
saying the theater of today owes a lot to technology, but I
really don't understand that. What technology could he be
talking about? And does it apply to such things as cosmetics
and stage makeup, or lighting or what? They certainly don't
use computers in the theater, do they? Is there any way of
finding out whether most of that technology is from the United
States or from foreign countries?

Q. I have to do some research about the Community Theater movement in the United States. As part of that, I want
to find out when the movement as such actually began, and
whether or not it is still going on on any large scale. I know
of a few cities that still have community theaters, but what
I'm wondering is where I could find a list, if one exists, of
all the theaters that were begun as part of that movement?
And I guess I will also need to find a list of all theaters
that are still in operation. Is there any sort of national organization of community theaters, or do they all pretty much
operate independently of one another? How could I find out
who funds these theaters? Are they usually funded by the
communities in which they exist, or do they get a lot of federal or state funds?

R. For a film-making course which I'm taking, our instructor wants us to find out something about the history of success of independent filmmakers. You know, people who have
made films that were not funded by the major studios in this
country. He said he wasn't sure if we could find all the information in one book or not; that we might have to use some
magazines and newspapers to get at the information. Basically, what he wants us to do is make a list of the ten most
successful films made by any filmmaker in the United States.
What we have to list is who made the film, who directed it,
how much it cost to produce the film, and how much money
was made in profit. Where could I go to find this information?

S. I'm interested in finding out a little bit about propaganda

films that were made during World War II. Where could I
find a list of films that the U. S. government made during
that time period which were essentially propaganda? Were
any of the films that the government made shown in regular
movie houses around the country, or were they viewed primarily by people in the military? Did Hollywood do anything
to help the government in the production of these films? Or
were some of the full-length feature films which Hollywood
made during that period controlled by anybody in the government? If so, who?

T. For my high school home economics class, our teacher
wants us to go back through magazines for the last fifty years,
and find pictures of what the average woman wore in the
course of a normal day. We are going to begin the sewing
section of our course in two weeks, and she wants us to be
able to compare what we wear today with what was worn in
the past. In addition to finding the pictures, she said she
also wants us to try to find out how many textiles exist today that did not exist ten or twenty or fifty years ago, so
that we can understand why clothes can now be designed and
sewn differently than they once were. Where can I find out
what those textiles are? and the pictures, too?

THEATER ARTS

Case Studies

I. Each student in Mr. Sweeney's theater course at Cimaron High School has to give a twenty-minute presentation on some aspect of stagecraft and/or staging. Jane Epperson has decided that she would like to do a project on costume design and construction. Since the senior class play this year will be Thornton Wilder's Our Town, she thought she might use that as an example of a specific task in costume design. For her speech, she would also like to be able to show illustrations of various productions of the play, as well as citing any instances of awards which were presented for costume design. To which sources of information would you direct her to locate answers to the following questions?

How many Broadway or off-Broadway productions of Our Town have been staged since the play was written?

Have they all basically used the same costume design?

Is there any way of finding out how many productions have been staged anywhere in the United States?

Who currently owns copyright to the play?

Who currently owns performance license to the play?

Has Our Town ever won any awards?

Have the costumes for any of the productions of Our Town ever won any awards?

Where could I locate photographs of different productions of Our Town?

Where could I locate lists of which designers have done the costumes for any of the Broadway productions of Our Town?

Where could I locate critics' remarks about any of the Broadway or off-Broadway productions of <u>Our Town</u>?

Do you think that it might be possible to find any critics' remarks about other productions around the country?

Where could I locate a list of technical terms which pertain to costume design and construction?

Since this is the first oral report that I have ever made, I think that it might be helpful to read about how to give an oral report. Do you know which one might be a good book?

Because the report must go for twenty minutes, and I have to write everything down ahead of time--where could I look to find out how many words people normally speak in one minute?

I might want to go into a little bit of history about costume design and how it related to the theater in the past. Do you have any good books about that subject?

II.   You know, I have been watching a lot of television lately, especially the late movies; and one thing that has really hit me is the different kinds of men that you see in Hollywood movies from different periods.   It's that whole idea of macho, of the he-man male.   In some ways there doesn't seem to have been a whole lot of change--like attitude.   But in other ways, like appearance, there really is a definite difference.

Do you know if anybody has done any research about this subject?   I'm not even sure what it might be called as a subject.   Possibly the image of the macho man in Hollywood movies?

I suppose that there really are a lot of different images of the macho male in Hollywood--like the cowboy, and the muscleman, and the gangster, and the hoodlum, and the rebel, and the soldier.   Hmmm ... do you think that it might be possible to find a list of those different images somewhere? And try to figure out certain time periods when certain images were most common?

Like the cowboy.   It doesn't seem like there are as many cowboy movies made today as there used to be.   Why is that? I guess I think it is because there just are not that many men around who want to be cowboys. But I'd like to find out what some experts might think about that.

Maybe I could find some articles in a few magazines about Hollywood and how it has portrayed men in movies? But how would I go about finding the magazines? If I use something like Readers' Guide, what would I look under?

Was Valentino the first real image of the macho man in movies? Or was there someone else who women swooned over?

I wonder ... do you think that any old Hollywood magazines ever did any popularity polls of their readers to find out who their readers thought were the most virile or manly men? How could I find out if something like that exists?

What about books? In my bookstore, I see a lot of books about Hollywood, but most of them are pretty much about one or two particular stars, and just talk about all the films of those arts. What I want is something that talks more about just male stars in general and how Hollywood has portrayed the male on the screen. Do you know if any books like that exist?

Are there any studies in psychology that might have been written about the effects of the image of the Hollywood male on how the American male views himself?

III. Our local theater group is planning to stage at least four, maybe five, plays next season. And we want to do something a little non-traditional for at least a few of them. One of the plays we know is going to be a Shakespeare play, probably either Hamlet or Macbeth. Well, since so much is being done experimentally with costuming, we thought that it would be a little bit different if we did the costuming using science fiction fashion. You know, dress the characters like they might be from "Star Trek" or some show like that.

Well, before we go too far into this, we want to locate some examples of what has been done before, in terms of costuming for either Hamlet or Macbeth. Is there any place I could find photographs of costumes that have been used in well-known productions of either play?

I personally think that it is important to get some criticism of those costumes as well. But I have no idea where I might find that. When critics review a play, do they usually include some sort of criticism of the costumes, too? Well, anyway, how could I find something along that line?

Once we have that information, we will know if anybody has done any productions using futuristic or science fiction costuming. But I would also like to find some illustrations of just plain old science fiction or futuristic dress, you know, like the costumes they use on television. Where could I find some of these? And I need them for men, women, and children.

In addition to what you see on television, it would probably be a good idea for us to look at some illustrated science fiction books, to get some other ideas about how people are going to dress in the future. Are there any science fiction books that have a lot of illustrations, or are those going to be really hard to find?

Maybe I'd be better off to look at some science fiction books for kids, huh? Don't they usually have a lot more illustrations than the ones they print for adults?

Finally, and I think maybe you won't be able to help me with this, but do you think that there is any way I could find a pattern for making a few science fiction-type clothes? Like an astronaut costume? Or a spaceman, or something like that? I just know this project is going to be a lot of work!

IV. I've been taking dance lessons now for something close to nine years; but it just struck me the other day that I really know next to nothing about certain kinds of dances and dancing. I came down here to the library to see what you all might have on the subject of dances and dancing among American Indians. I'm sure that there must be something written about the subject somewhere, but I just don't know where to look.

I did read one of the encyclopedias that you have here. And the article they had on Indians was interesting. It did mention dances, but never really got into anything too specific. What I want to know, first of all, are the different types of dances that American Indians once had.

I've heard of things like fertility dances and rain dances and things like that, but they must have had a lot more dances that don't get as much attention. Were there different types or kinds of dances among the Indians? I mean, were certain dances done only for religious purposes, and other dances done to help the crops grow?

I guess I just want to read everything I can about this subject. I'd really like to know who did the dancing, too. Was it the men and the women and the children? Or were only certain people allowed to do these dances?

And did the Indians have anybody like a dance master? Someone who would lead them in all the dances?

I wonder, did they believe that dances were magical at all? Or that dancing in general was magical?

And were all of their dances done for a specific reason, or was there anything like popular dance among the Indians ... where they just danced to have a good time, and for no other reason?

Did they have to wear certain kinds of clothes or costumes for certain dances? If they did, did the costumes have any meaning for the dance, or were they just worn for color?

Did most of the tribes have the same dances? Or did each tribe pretty much devise its own dances and reasons for dancing?

I would really like to be able to find some photographs or at least good illustrations of some of the Indian dances, as well as some explanation of choreography, if there was any. Where do you think that I might be able to find that?

Did dancing, in general, mean a lot to the American Indian? What I mean is, was it a really important part of American Indian life? Were there any gods of dance or dancing that the Indians prayed to, or performed for?

Are there any sorts of records about the success rate of certain types of dances, like fertility or rain dances? What I mean is, did it usually rain when rain dances were done? Or did people become pregnant after fertility dances?

Are a lot of the old Indian dances still done today by the tribes which still remain?

INTERDISCIPLINARY SEARCH PROBLEMS

INTERDISCIPLINARY

Search Problems

A. I really am puzzled about a couple things, and I don't
know exactly where to go to find an answer. Maybe you can
help me. Lately, I've been bothered by the whole question
of morality and immorality. I've been talking to a friend
about it, but we can't seem to reach any sort of agreement.
She says that the notions of morality and immorality are just
theoretical philosophical arguments. Well, I think that they
are really religious issues. I agree that there is some philosophy behind the issues, but that you can't talk about either
one without talking about religion. Basically, what I want to
know is, can somebody live what is considered to be an im-
moral life, and still be religious? I don't think that they can;
but my friend says she knows a lot of people who do.

B. I want to get at some material which talks about music
and what music is, or should be. But what I want is some
stuff that will tell me something about the past as well as
the present. Like what I want to know is, have people always thought that good music was good music, no matter
what the time period was? For instance, when people said
that something was good music in the 17th century, was what
they meant the same thing that people meant when they said
that something was good music during the 18th century? Or
the 19th century? Or today? And who really determines
what is good music or what is bad music? Is it generally
the composers of the times, or is it the critics?

C. I'd like to find something about the personal philosophies
of four different artists of the 20th century: Jasper Johns,
Mark Rothko, Jackson Pollock, and Andy Warhol. They are
all pretty much representative of different kinds of art of the
20th century. But I'm wondering exactly how different their
philosophies of art really are. And I would also be interested
in finding out exactly how well each of these artists managed

to display or communicate their philosophies through their
art. Has there been very much written about this? Where
would be a good place to start looking?

D. I want to know if there has been a whole lot written
about the philosophy of theater. Not about drama, but about
theater. What I mean is, has anybody actually stated what
kind of experience people should have when they go to the
theater? Like the kind of physical environment that they
should be in? There really are a lot of different kinds of
theaters and theater buildings around. Those that are outside and surrounded by lots of gardens and green. Those that
are outside and have nothing at all in terms of environment.
And then there are lots of different kinds of indoor theaters
and stages. I guess what I'm asking is what determines how
a theater will be built? Is it basically built for actors and
acting? Or is the audience given pretty high consideration
in the final plans?

E. A friend of mine recently told me that she had overheard
some people talking about the influence of religion upon music,
and the term "rasta" was repeated throughout their conversa-
tion. She was quite confused because she thought that the
term was either Italian or Spanish; but the people using it
kept referring to something called "regay" music and to someone with the last name of Helassie or Selassie or something
like that. I don't really know how you spell either term or
name or whatever they are. From which language does the
term "rasta" come? I think it's Italian, but my friend said
it was not. What is the connection between this term and
regay music. What kind of music is it? Does it have any
religious significance? And who is that person that they kept
talking about? Is he a musician? What does he have to do
with "rasta" or with regay music?

F. My aunt just returned from Europe on some sort of tour
of the great cathedrals of France and Germany, and is just
enamored with all the stained-glass windows which she saw
while she was there. She wants me to find out how they
made those windows and who made them, especially the windows in Paris and Cologne. Where could I find out who the
artist was who made the windows for Notre-Dame Cathedral
in Paris? Did he just design them, or did he actually take
part in making the glass as well? Do you have any books
that explain how they achieved all those beautiful blues and
reds? Did they just have to add dye to the glass? Also,
how long does it take to make a stained-glass window like

the ones you see in churches? And what do they do if they
make a mistake? How long have people been doing stained-
glass? Is it very expensive to do?

G. I've been thinking about a term paper topic for a 20th-
century comparative literature course. Last year I read
Beckett's Waiting for Godot; and the professor has talked
some about existentialism and 20th-century continental literature. This year I've read Sartre's Nausea and Camus' The
Stranger, and I became interested in the philosophical aspects
of the two novels. Did Camus ever have any direct contact
with Sartre? Did he ever write any explicitly philosophical
works? Did Sartre or Camus ever write any critical essays
on each other's fiction? Also, I was wondering where I
could find a brief list of basic philosophical works by Sartre
and others on existentialism. One other problem--I don't read
French as well as I need to, so I'd prefer reading stuff that
is written in English.

H. I want to locate something that talks about the Bible not
as a religious work, but as a work of literature. What I
want to know, for instance, is something about some of the
major characters that appear in the Bible. Do they exist in
other religious works, too? Somebody said that a lot of the
characters in the Bible are the same characters that you can
find in some of the folklore and folk literature of other cultures. Is that really true? Has there been any sort of literary criticism of the Bible? Like whether it has a good
plot? What the basic themes are? And how good the char-
acter development is?

I. I'm interested in locating some really good examples of
music that has been written for and performed by religious
choirs and choruses. Is that very hard to do? I don't really
want to get into stuff like gospel music or hoedown-type music. More like Handel's Messiah. Where can I find something that will tell me about the different kinds of major pieces
of religious vocal music, like Handel's Messiah? Is much of
this sort of thing being written today, or is most of it from
older times? I also want to listen to some of it, to get some
idea of how it all compares. Is it still possible to get some
really good recordings of this type of music? How am I
going to know which are the best recordings?

J. I am doing some research for a term paper for one of
my art history courses, and I seem to be coming across a
lot of information that gets at the influence of the Christian

Church on the fine arts in general, especially during the
Middle Ages and the Renaissance. What I would like to
know, if you can find it, is exactly who controlled that influence over the fine arts, especially painting. What I mean
is, was it the popes, or some other officials in the various
churches? Is there any way of finding out which pope had
the most influence on the arts? Did the Vatican ever issue
any statements or directives saying what an artist could or
could not paint? Or what they should or should not paint?

K. I want to find out what kind of textile art exists in religion. You know, things that are of a religious nature or
subject matter which are entirely made from different fibers
and textiles? Like I'm sure there must be a whole lot of
macrame being done with religious subjects. And even stuff
like silkscreening onto cloth. But what about things like
quilts, and tapestries, and rugs, and other types of weaving?
Are there any of these things in existence which are considered to be truly great works of art in their own right? Are
there any collections of photographs or prints of these things
that I might be able to look at? Even some slides would
help.

L. I want to find out something about these two types of
plays called miracle plays and mystery plays. Apparently
they were some sort of religious plays that were written during the Middle Ages. But I don't know much more than that.
What I want to know is what was the difference between the
two kinds of plays. And also where they were performed,
or even if they were performed. Were they performed in
churches or in theaters? And were they popular at all with
the audiences? Who were the major authors of miracle plays
and mystery plays? Were they written by priests, or by regular people? Were there any difficulties in the actual staging
of the plays?

M. Would it be possible to find out what the relationship has
been between religion and medicine over the centuries? I
guess what I want to know is which one was around first, and
whether the two fields have ever really been one. People like
witch doctors and medicine men are really operating in both
fields, aren't they? I guess I always thought that religion was
more concerned with the salvation of the soul, and medicine
with the body. But has religion ever been concerned with the
salvation of the body? Or medicine with the soul?

N. I keep seeing so many reproductions of works of art, and

it got me to wondering about copyright. Can works of art be copyrighted? Do they have to be copyrighted? Or should they be copyrighted? Are there limitations as to the kind of art that one can copyright? And who generally holds copyright over a work of art? Is it the artist or the person who bought the work of art? And what about prints or reproductions? Can a company that takes a photograph of a piece of sculpture from a certain angle copyright that photograph so that no one else will use it without paying them royalties? Does an artist generally have the same protection under copyright that an author does?

O. I want to locate some information about political literature in Nazi Germany before and during World War II. Basically, I want to find out what were the most popular novels and short stories of that time period. That is, the favorite ones among the German people. What I also would like to know is how well these works of literature actually reflected the politics of Germany at the time. Have a lot of these works been translated into English? Are they the type of thing that I could buy at my local bookstore? And finally, where could I find some good literary criticism of these works, as well as criticism written from a political point of view?

P. It is pretty well known that more than a few authors have claimed that the inspiration for some of their major works has flowed straight out of a bottle, usually one containing some sort of alcoholic beverage. But what about musicians? I think it is fairly common for most rock musicians to be involved with drugs of one sort or another, isn't it? Well, leaving them aside, what I really want to know is how many great composers and musicians have openly admitted, as some authors have done, that their primary inspiration has come from some mind-altering substance, whether that be booze or drugs or whatever? Were there any great composers who were, in fact, drug addicts?

Q. One of my instructors mentioned the other day that there were museums and libraries of erotica in this country. Well, I did not believe him and so I went off to check some directory of special collections or something like that that said that there were. My God, what is the world coming to! Well, I want to know more about these places. I mean, what kind of things do they have in them? Stuff like dirty pictures and sculptures and stuff like that? Or is it mainly books? I never saw a great work of art that was erotic. They certainly don't have any works by the really famous artists, do they?   Or is that the sort of thing that they never tell you about in art history courses?   Do any of these places have picture catalogs of the stuff that they have?   Do they allow children into these places?

R.   It seems to me that nudity in the theater and in films is almost commonplace now; that you can almost expect to see it no matter what you go to, except maybe a Disney film. But I don't understand why that is.   How long has it been since the first real instance of nudity in either film or theater?   Aren't there any sorts of codes of ethics among the movie industry or the theater industry?   Have these codes been altered to allow nudity on stage and in film?   In how many states in this country can a theater be shut down or a movie house closed for allowing a public display of nudity? Have there been any plays that have been completely acted in the nude?   Where was that?

S.   Where could I get some information on the history and design of the yo-yo?   I've seen all sorts of neat yo-yos in stores, and I'm sure that there must be some that are really ornate and maybe even jeweled.   A friend of mine has a silver yo-yo that was made about ten years ago, but that is really the only special kind I've seen.   Has anybody done anything like a pictorial history of the yo-yo?   Are there any "royal" yo-yos around, or is playing with a yo-yo not considered a fit thing for royalty to do?

T.   I'd like to find some information about the types of shows that used to be staged in saloons in the Old West.   On television shows and in the movies, they usually show a lot of women dancing and some guy playing the piano.   Is that a fairly accurate portrayal of how things really were at that time?   Did most saloons have the same general kind of entertainment?   And where could I find something about how the townspeople in general reacted to these places?   Did they consider them sinful, or just another form of entertainment? Of all the saloons of the Old West, which is the most famous? And who were the most famous female performers?   Who was Lola Montez?

APPENDIX

The following examples are provided as possible,
rather than definitive, solutions to three selected
search problems. Grateful acknowledgment is
made to Anne Johnson, Mary Leatherwood, and
William Muehlbauer for their agreement to allow
publication of these exercises.

LITERATURE

Search Problem

R. I would like to find some information about some of the
kings and knights and queens and ladies that appear in a lot
of medieval writing. People like King Arthur and the Knights
of the Round Table; and Guinevere, and Robin Hood and Maid
Marion. Were these people real people? I mean, did they
actually live? Is there any way to find out what was the first
book that they were mentioned in? I have noticed that their
names come up a lot in Romantic literature, but I wonder if
people from other time periods wrote about them. Is there
any way to find out, for instance, in how many novels King
Arthur and Queen Guinevere appear? Or whether all those
novels were in the English language?

SOLUTION
by Anne Johnson

Questions:

1) Were King Arthur, Guinevere, the Knights of the Round
    Table, Robin Hood, and Maid Marian real people? If
    so, did they really do the things credited to them?

155

A.   Strategy:
Source: literary encyclopedia or dictionary
Entry terms: "Arthur," "Guinevere," "Knights of the
Round Table," "Maid Marian," "Robin Hood."

B.   Search:
Benet, William Rose.   The Reader's Encyclopedia.
2nd ed. 1965.
S. v. "Arthur," "Guinevere," "Knights of the Round
Table," "Maid Marian," "Robin Hood."
   Pertinent information reveals that Robin Hood, Guinevere, and the Knights of the Round Table were legen-
dary figures.   Identifies "Arthur" as a Celtic chieftain
of the sixth century.   There is no pertinent information
on Maid Marian in Benet, and I have not located a sat-
isfactory answer in any other source.

Collier's Encyclopedia.   1978 ed.
S. v. "Robin Hood."
   This article reports evidence for an historical
Robin (Robert) Hood, but this cannot be substantiated.

Encyclopedia Americana.   International edition.   1977.
S. v. "Arthurian Romances."
   Pertinent information regarding Arthur.

2)   In which books were the characters first mentioned?

A.   Search strategy:
Source: literary encyclopedia or dictionary
Entry terms: each name, as in #1

B.   Search:
Benet, William Rose.   The Reader's Encyclopedia.
2nd ed. 1965.
S. v. "Arthur."   Cross-reference to "Arthurian legend."
S. v. "Arthurian legend."
S. v. "Round Table."
S. v. "Robin Hood."
S. v. "Robin Hood: The May Games, the Robin Hood
Plays, and the Morris Dance."
   Each entry provides pertinent information.   I found
no reference to Guinevere's initial appearance on the
literary scene in any of the sources consulted.

3) These characters are often mentioned in Romantic literature, but are they written about in other periods?

    A. Search strategy:
    Source: literary encyclopedia
    Entry term: each name

    B. Search:
    Benet, William Rose. The Reader's Encyclopedia.
    2nd ed. 1965.
    S. v. "Arthurian legend. "
    S. v. "Robin Hood. "
    Each entry contains pertinent information.

    Subject Guide to Books in Print, 1979-1980.
    S. v. "Robin Hood. "
    Sixteen current titles are entered.

4) Is there any way to find out in how many novels Arthur and Guinevere appear?

    A. Search strategy:
    Source: Subject Guide to Books in Print: Cumulative Book Index.
    Entry term: "Arthur. "

    B. Search:
    Fiction Catalog. 8th ed. 1977.
    S. v. "Arthur, King. "
    Eight titles are listed.
    S. v. "Guinevere. " No entry. It was listed under "Guenevere, Queen. "
    Five titles are listed.

    C. Comments:
    I feel as though there must be a source somewhere which would answer this inquiry, but I could not locate it.

    On this particular search problem, since I was reporting in written form, it would have been less confusing if I had broken #1, #2, and #3 into five parts each to cover each character separately rather than collectively.

THEATER ARTS

Search Problem

H. Me and a few of my friends are planning a Halloween
party and we decided that we want people to come dressed
in any costume from the period between World War I and
World War II. Well, the problem with that is that not everybody we have invited knows what people used to dress like
then. So I'm here to find some books and magazines that
might have lots and lots of pictures of how people looked at
that time. Do you have any books here that would be really
good to use? And what about magazine titles? Which magazines would be the best ones, or at least have the most pictures of fashions from that period?

SOLUTION
     by Mary Leatherwood

Questions:

1) Are there books which contain pictures of clothing styles
    between approximately 1920 and 1939?

    A. Strategy:
        Source: Card catalog check under "Costume" and
        "Clothing and Dress"
            Check index or table of contents for treatment of the
        years in question.

    B. Search:
            Bearing in mind that so-called "high fashion" and
        clothing actually worn during a particular period may
        vary greatly, attempt to find examples of both.

    In the order consulted:

    # Boucher, Francois Leon Louis. 20,000 Years of Fashion:
       The History of Costume and Personal Adornment. 1967.
       Table of Contents--Chapter XII: "Costume Fashions from
       1920." Pp. 411-415.
           Emphasis is on French "high fashion."

─────────────────
May be useful; patron must decide.

Payne, Blanche. History of Costume: From the
Ancient Egyptians to the Twentieth Century. 1965.
  Stops in the early 1900's.

Bruhn, Wolfgang. A Pictorial History of Costume.
1955.
  Stops at the end of the 19th century.

Wilcox, R. Turner. The Dictionary of Costume.
1969.
  Contains some information under "Twentieth Century"
(Pp. 363-368)--women's styles, mostly underwear, neg-
ligee, corsets, and swim wear. Men's styles must be
found in pages of pictures divided by type of clothing
rather than by year (pp. 374, 376-78). Refers to author's other work: Five Centuries of American Costume.

* Monro, Isabel. The Costume Index. 1937.
   S. v. "United States." See reference to "Twentieth
   Century." Citations are for years before 1920. However, the 1957 Supplement is useful and refers the
   reader to plates in many books:
   S. v. "Twentieth Century" with subheadings:
   "1920-1930" (31 possible sources)
   "1930-1940" (25 possible sources)

* Wilcox, R. Turner. Five Centuries of American Costume. 1963.
     Contents--see: "20th Century" with subheadings
   "1920-1930" and "1930-1940. "
     Pages 161-167 are text. Pictures have no page
   numbers and are labeled "Twentieth Century--1920's. "

Kerr, R. N. 100 Years of Costumes in America.
   1951.
     Contains a few good pictures.

* Women's Wear Daily. Sixty Years of Fashion, 1900-
   1960: The Evolution of Women's Styles in America.
   1963.
     Good for women's fashions.

* Kybalová, Ludmila; Herbenová, Olga; and Lamarová,
   Milena. The Pictorial Encyclopedia of Fashion. 1968.

*Could be recommended to patron.

Contents: "Between the Wars 1918-1939." Again, contains only women's fashions.

* Schoeffler, O. E. and Gale, William. Esquire's Encyclopedia of 20th Century Men's Fashions. 1973.
Access for specific dates possible only through skimming dated illustrations in categorical groupings. For instance, "Suits," "Sports Jackets," etc.

* Moore, Doris Langley. Fashion Through Fashion Plates: 1771-1970. 1971.
Pages 156-168 treat women's fashions for this period.

C. Comments:
1920-1939 chosen because most sources divide into decades, and these years are close to the actual dates encompassing the between-war years.

Some back-tracking was necessary in the search (which does not show here) because of the separation of our libraries and card catalogs.

Women's fashions are much more easily found than men's fashions.

Entire 20th century is often treated as a unit.

Previous experience looking up this sort of question allowed general encyclopedia articles to be largely eliminated--except as a last resort--because they tend to illustrate the more unusual earlier dress styles.

2) Are there periodicals which contain pictures of clothing styles between approximately 1920 and 1939?

A. Strategy:
Check periodical indexes.
Possible source: General periodicals of the period, especially the "picture" magazines (Life, Look, etc.).

B. Search:
International Index to Periodicals: Devoted Chiefly to the Humanities and Science.
Forerunner of Social Science and Humanities Index.

S. v. "Fashion," "Clothing and Dress," "Costume."
Not particularly useful. Periodicals indexed are not likely to be readily available.

Readers' Guide to Periodical Literature.
S. v. "Clothing and Dress"
Refers to a variety of periodicals and indicates those which are illustrated.

Simple examination of any periodicals one may have from the period in question--some are more likely to have pictures than others (Life, Look, news magazines, Good Housekeeping, Ladies' Home Journal, etc.

C. Comments:
Success of the last possibility is, of course, contingent on one's library owning copies from 1920-1940.

Books seem a much more easily-reachable source for an essentially casual question about party costumes. A more thorough periodical search might be justified for play costumes.

MUSIC

Search Problem

Q. I am interested in finding out what, if anything, is being done in the field of music therapy. Has anyone, particularly musicians, written anything about what sort of applications can be made with music to the therapeutic setting? Is any music therapy being done by musicians rather than by professional psychologists or psychiatrists? I would also like to know if there are any musical recordings which have been made expressly for therapeutic use. Who are the most important people writing in this field today?

SOLUTION
by William Muehlbauer

Questions:

1) Information, general, on music therapy and what is being done in the field.

A.   Search strategy:
Source: Index: Music Index; Readers' Guide to Per-
iodical Literature; Music Therapy Index.
Entry term: "Music Therapy. "

B.   Search:
Music Index.
S. v. "Music Therapy. " Cross-referenced to "Therapy,
Music. " Readers' Guide to Periodical Literature.
S. v. "Music Therapy. " Music Therapy Index. 1976.
S. v. "Music Therapy. "
Pertinent information in all three indexes.

2)   Have musicians written anything about the application of
music to the therapeutic setting?

A.   Search strategy:
Source: Index: Music Index.
Entry term: "Therapy, Music. "

Source: Index: Music Therapy Index.
Entry term: "Music Composition. "

B.   Search:
Music Index.
S. v. "Therapy, Music. "
Contains citations to pertinent information.
Music Therapy Index.
S. v. "Music Composition. "
Citations to information are provided.

3)   Is there any music therapy being done by musicians?

A.   Search strategy:
Source: Index: Music Therapy Index.
Entry term: "Musicians. "

B.   Search:
Music Therapy Index.
S. v. "Musicians. "
Has relevant citations.

4)   Where can one find musical recordings made for music
therapy?

A. Search strategy:
    Source: card catalog
    Entry term: "Music Therapy. "

B. Search:
    Card Catalog.
    Subject Heading: "Music Therapy. "
    Ward, David. Hearts, Hands & Voices. 1976.
       Contains a list of recordings made specifically for
    a music therapy setting. Pp. 84-85.

5) Who are the most important people writing in this field
    today?

    A. Search strategy:
        Source: Index: Music Therapy Index.

    B. Search:
        Music Therapy Index.
           I believe this index gives a representation of those au-
        thors notable in the various sections of music therapy.